The valley of

Arthur Preston Hankins

Alpha Editions

This edition published in 2024

ISBN : 9789362091437

Design and Setting By
Alpha Editions
www.alphaedis.com
Email - info@alphaedis.com

As per information held with us this book is in Public Domain.
This book is a reproduction of an important historical work. Alpha Editions uses the best technology to reproduce historical work in the same manner it was first published to preserve its original nature. Any marks or number seen are left intentionally to preserve its true form.

Contents

CHAPTER I AN EXTRA BED ....- 1 -
CHAPTER II EL TRONO DE TOLERANCIA ....- 6 -
CHAPTER III THE PROSPECTOR'S STORY........................- 11 -
CHAPTER IV A MEMBER OF THE CLAN ....- 16 -
CHAPTER V THE CONFERENCE AT JORNY SPRINGS...- 20 -
CHAPTER VI SECOND SIGHT ....- 26 -
CHAPTER VII LOT'S WIFE AND SHIRTTAIL HENRY......- 33 -
CHAPTER VIII MISSING...- 39 -
CHAPTER IX A CASE FOR REJUVENATION ....- 44 -
CHAPTER X SHIRTTAIL BEND...- 49 -
CHAPTER XI THE TRAIL TO MOSQUITO ....- 56 -
CHAPTER XII THE LAND OF QUEER DELIGHTS............- 61 -
CHAPTER XIII AT TWO IN THE CAÑON...........................- 68 -
CHAPTER XIV THE LONG STRAW ....- 77 -
CHAPTER XV VAGRANCY CAÑON......................................- 82 -
CHAPTER XVI THE CAMP IN VAGRANCY CAÑON ....- 87 -
CHAPTER XVII BEAR PASS..- 93 -
CHAPTER XVIII IN THE PALM OF THE MOUNTAINS..- 101 -
CHAPTER XIX RIDDLES ....- 107 -
CHAPTER XX THE INTERIM OF DOUBTS ....- 113 -
CHAPTER XXI THE CAVE OF HYPOCRITICAL FROGS..- 119 -
CHAPTER XXII DR. SHONTO RIDES ALONE ....- 125 -
CHAPTER XXIII OLD ACQUAINTANCES ....- 131 -
CHAPTER XXIV MARY CHOOSES A SEAT ....- 135 -
CHAPTER XXV THE DEADLY BULL AND THE SILVER FOX..- 141 -

CHAPTER XXVI THE LAST TABLET ....- 147 -
CHAPTER XXVII ADRIFT ON LOST RIVER.....................- 154 -
CHAPTER XXVIII THE MESSAGE ....- 160 -

CHAPTER I
AN EXTRA BED

TRIED outlanders though they were, Dr. Inman Shonto and Andy Jerome were hopelessly lost. Afoot, horseback, and by motor car the pair had covered thousands of square miles of desert and forest land in Southern California. But it was different up here in the mountainous region of the northern part of the state, where they found themselves surrounded by heavy timber vaster than they had dreamed could have been left standing by the ensanguined hand of the lumberman. And, besides, thin fingers of fog were reaching in from the sea, about eighteen miles to the west of them.

For hours they had been following wooded ridges, which here and there offered a view of the seemingly illimitable sweep of redwood forests below them. Spruce, fir, several varieties of oak, and madrones crowned these ridges—trees of a height and girth that they could understand. But down below them towered the monarchs of the vegetable kingdom, straight as the path of righteousness, solemn, aloof—impossible trees—whose height would bring their tops on a level with the clock of the Metropolitan Building, whose boles occupied a space greater than a good-sized living room.

They awed the southerners immeasurably, for this was their first trip into the northern part of their state. They were silent as they hurried on, sliding down steep slopes, clambering up rocky, timbered inclines, always hoping for some familiar object that would show them they were on the campward trail.

Each carried a .25-.35 rifle, for they had left camp early that morning to hunt deer—and both had entertained fond hopes that a wandering bear or a panther might cross their path. The doctor had wounded a big six-pointer close to noon, and following the bloody trail which the cripple left had led the pair astray.

Now night was close at hand, and, for all they knew, they were still many miles from camp. The trail had inveigled them down into the mysteries of the dark forest below them, and there they had lost all sense of direction. With the approach of night they had abandoned the bloody trail and climbed to the ridges once more, in the hope of relocating themselves. But an hour had passed, and they still were lost.

"This is a little serious, Andy," remarked the doctor. "I'm afraid we haven't much of an idea as to the vast scope of this forest. Of course we'll make it back sometime, and I guess we're old enough hands at the game to take care of ourselves until we do; but meanwhile we're going to be up against a little inconvenience, to put it mildly."

"It's going to be mighty cold to-night," was the only answer that the younger man vouchsafed.

He was about twenty-four, this companion of the doctor—a good-looking youth with light curly hair and a friendly blue eye. He was of medium height, well knit, wiry. His step was light and his muscles sure, and more than once the older man eyed him admiringly as they hurried on into the coming dusk.

Dr. Inman Shonto was one of those men who command attention wherever they go. He was tall and lean and broad-shouldered, and his outing clothes had been fitted to his remarkable body with precision. He was an ugly man as masculine comeliness goes, but, for all that, women found him intensely interesting. His nose was monstrous, and lightly pitted from bridge to tip. His mouth was big, and the lips were thick, puckered, and firm. His hair was thin and neutral in colour—somewhere between a dark brown and a light. His ears were rather large and a trifle outstanding. His eyes were grey and very intense in their manner of observing others.

It was the strong face of a strong man. One knew instinctively that great will power was this man's heritage. One believed, after a glance into that homely face, that this man took what he wanted from life, and that his wants were by no means puny. Even in hunting clothes Dr. Inman Shonto was fastidious. And his walk was fastidious, even here in the wilderness. The realization that he and his young companion were lost in the wilds did not serve to ruffle the doctor's calm exterior. He was nothing if not self-controlled on all occasions.

Despite his homeliness, his smile was engaging as he turned and looked back at Andy after topping a little bald rise toward which the two had been travelling, hoping on its summit to gain a better view of the surrounding country.

"Andy," he said, "I smell smoke. Sound encouraging?"

The young man reached his side, and the two stood looking in every direction and sniffing speculatively.

"I get it, too, Doctor," Andy told the other finally. "It seems to be over in that direction."

Andy pointed west, and the doctor nodded silently.

"There's a ranch or a camp pretty close," he decided. "Now let's locate that smoke definitely and make a bee-line for it. I don't just fancy a night in this cold, unfriendly forest."

"Do you know, Dr. Shonto," said Andy, "that I don't exactly think of the forest as unfriendly. Time and again, when you and I have been together in the outlands, you've thought nature unkind—bleak—unfriendly. Nature never strikes me that way."

"That's your inheritance from your Alps-climbing Swiss ancestors, I imagine," replied the doctor. "But, if you'll pardon me, Andrew, I'm more interested right now in locating a welcoming curl of blue smoke over the treetops than I am in a discussion of the attitude of Mother Nature toward two of her misplaced atoms. Look over there to the west. (I suppose that's west.) Don't you imagine you see a thin stream of smoke going up over there—just above that massive bull pine on the brow of that hill? Confound this infernal fog!"

"Yes, I believe you're right," Andy agreed after looking a long time in the direction the doctor had indicated. And after another pause—"Yes, smoke, all right. And if it weren't for the fog it would spread, and we'd never have seen it. Now what, Doctor?"

Dr. Shonto gave the surrounding country careful study.

"It seems to me," he decided, "that, if we head straight for that tall fir on the brow of the hill beyond the next one, we ought to see what's causing the smoke. But we've got to go down and up, down and up; and we'll pass through heavy timber between here and there. We must keep our wits about us and not swerve from a straight line. And that's hard to do, with the fog rolling in on us. Anyway, it's up to us to try it. Let's go!"

With each of them picking his own way, they rattled down steep slopes and came upon tiny creeks, cold, brown from the dye of fallen autumn leaves. They clambered up slopes that seemed far steeper because of the extra strain they put upon their hearts and muscles. Dense growths of chaparral occasionally confronted them and made them make detours, despite their firm resolve to keep to the straight and narrow way. But in half an hour after sighting the thin stream of smoke they came out in an open space on a hillside and saw the tall fir which was their goal.

They crossed to it on level land, to look down a more precipitous slope than they had before encountered. And down there far below them they saw the misty gleam of cabin lights as they struggled with the night and the increasing obstinacy of the fog that marched in from the sea.

"Here's a sort of trail, Doctor," announced Andrew Jerome. "And it looks to be leading straight toward those lights. Shall we try it?"

"Sure," replied the doctor. "By all means. You're the better mountaineer, Andy—take the lead. We can get a shakedown on the floor of the man who made those lights, I guess, and get set on the right trail to-morrow morning."

It was dark now, and the insweeping fog added to the density of the surrounding gloom. Far to their left coyotes lifted their mocking, plaintive yodel to the Goddess of Darkness, their patron saint, who shielded their stealthy deviltry from the eyes of men. But the blurred lights beckoned the wanderers downward, and they obeyed the signal, slipping over rounded stones, staggering into prickly bushes, sliding over abrupt ledges.

Andrew Jerome followed the trail by instinct, and Dr. Shonto was glad to follow Andy. The youth's aptitude in the mountains was ever a source of wonder for the doctor, and often he had told the boy that he attributed it to heredity. For on his mother's side of the family Andy's ancestors had been of Alpine Swiss stock, by name Zanini. Dr. Inman Shonto was a firm believer in heredity, anyway, and his young friend's dexterous mountaineering presented a sound basis for his theorizing.

They came out eventually on level land, heavily timbered with pines. Straight through the pines the trail led them, and soon they were confronted by a set of bars. Beyond the bars the fog-screened lights still invited them, so the doctor lifted his voice and called.

There came no answer from the gloom. No dog rushed around an invisible cabin to challenge them.

"Let's take a chance, Andy," said the doctor. "If a pack of hounds leaps out at us, we can retreat as gracefully as possible. We've got to get closer to make ourselves heard."

They crawled between the bars and struck out along a beaten path. Still no outraged canine came catapulting toward them. Still the house remained invisible. Only the smeared lights stared at them through the fog.

Dr. Shonto came to a halt, and Andy stopped beside him.

"In the cabin there!" called Shonto. "Cabin ahoy!"

Several silent moments followed, and then, between the window lights that had lured them there, a new streak of muddy brilliancy grew to a rectangle, and a woman's figure stood framed by a door.

"Hello!" shouted the doctor. "We're lost in the woods and hunting shelter for the night. Our camp is far from here, and we can't find it. Can you help us out? There are two of us—two men! We'll gladly pay you for your inconvenience."

They saw the figure of the woman turn. She was speaking with somebody within the cabin, and her profile was toward them. It vanished as she once more turned her face their way.

"Come on in!" came her invitation. "She says she'll do the best she can for you."

"She," muttered the doctor. "I once knew a man that never called his wife anything but 'she.' Come on—I smell baking-powder biscuits, or my name's not Shonto. Here's the backwoods for you."

And then, as if to give the lie to his words, he stepped upon a broad stone doorstep and was faced by a radiant girl in a sky-blue evening gown, with precious stones in her dark hair, and gilded, high-heeled slippers on her feet.

"Good evening," she greeted them easily. "Welcome to El Trono de Tolerancia. There are baking powder biscuits, venison, and chocolate for supper, and we've an extra bed."

CHAPTER II
EL TRONO DE TOLERANCIA

DR. INMAN SHONTO was not easily moved to a display of surprise, but for at least once in his life he found himself unequal to the occasion.

The girl in the doorway was galvanically pretty. Her features were of that striking, contrasty quality that is the result of an artistic makeup—but she was not made up. She was dark, red-lipped, large-eyed, and her figure brought a quick flush of masculine appreciation in the doctor's face. Physically, it seemed to him, he had never before seen so gloriously all-right a girl. But the desirable physical characteristics which she displayed were not what had caused the cat to get the physician's tongue. It was the low-neck, sleeveless gown, the sparkling hair ornaments, the gilded slippers and the creaseless silk stockings—all of which had for their background the coal-oil-lighted interior of a log cabin lost in the wilderness—that had wrecked his customary poise.

Her ringing laugh served in a measure to readjust his scattered wits. She had interpreted the meaning of his surprise.

"It's my birthday!" was the girlish announcement that followed her fun-provoking laugh. "It's my birthday—and I'm twenty-two—and my name is Charmian Reemy. *Mrs.* Charmian Reemy, I suppose it is my duty to inform you. Aren't you coming in, Dr. Shonto?"

At last the doctor's hat was in his hand, and Andy Jerome, standing just behind him and equally amazed, removed his too.

Shonto was mumbling something about the unexpected pleasure of meeting a girl in the wilderness who knew his name while Andy followed him inside. The girl hurried on before them and was arranging comfortable thong-bottom chairs before a huge stone fireplace. Skins and bright-coloured Navajo rugs half covered the puncheon floor. Dainty, inexpensive curtains hung at the windows. Deer antlers and enlarged photographs of wildwood scenes broke the solemnity of the dark log walls.

Before the fireplace another woman bent and cooked in a Dutch oven on red coals raked one side from the roaring fire of fir wood.

"This is Mary Temple, my companion, nurse, cook, and adviser in all matters pertaining to my general welfare," announced the girl. "I love her companionship, appreciate her nursing, rave over her cooking, and ignore her advice entirely. Mary Temple, this is Dr. Inman Shonto, lost in the woods with a friend whom I have not given him time to introduce."

Once more the bombarded doctor stood by his guns, bowed gravely to middle-aged Mary Temple—who smiled over her lean shoulder but continued to hover her Dutch oven—then turned to Andy.

"Mrs. Reemy, permit me," he said. "My friend, Andrew Jerome."

"Mr. Jerome," laughed the girl, extending her hand, "I am happy to welcome you to my birthday party." Then, with one of her amazingly swift movements, she swung about to the physician. "And you, Dr. Shonto, are to be the guest of honour—and you are going to tell us all about glands and things like that."

"It is absolutely impossible," Dr. Shonto returned gallantly, "that I could have met you and forgotten you, Mrs. Reemy."

"Very well spoken, Doctor," she retorted, with a smile that twisted up a trifle at one corner of her mouth. "But I have heard that before. One would expect Dr. Inman Shonto, renowned gland specialist, to say something more original. There—I'm being impolite again! (Beat you to it that time, didn't I, Mary Temple!) But you are pardoned for a commonplace speech, Doctor. It must have stunned you not a little to come upon a dolled-up flapper out here in the forest. I'll relieve your mind instantly. We have never met before. But I have read about you for years. And this morning, when I was down at Lovejoy's for my mail—and incidentally a big piece of venison which I hadn't expected to be given me—I saw you and Mr. Jerome walking up the road with your guns. I inquired about you, and was told that the eminent Dr. Shonto and his friend Mr. Jerome, of Los Angeles, were in our midst. And, though I saw only your backs this morning, those shoulders of yours, Doctor, are as wide when seen from the front as from the rear. And when I saw them threatening to push to right and left the uprights of my door frame, I thought Samson was about to bring the house down on us two Philistines. For that's what we are, gentlemen—outlawed Philistines. And this is the house called El Trono de Tolerancia—which in Spanish is equivalent to The Throne of Tolerance. All right, Mary Temple—I see your shoulders quivering! I'll stop right now and let somebody else get in a word. But since I already know the doctor and his friend—and a great deal about the doctor that he doesn't suspect—doesn't it stand to reason that they ought to hear about us before sitting down to my birthday dinner?"

"You oughtn't to've called yourself a flapper," said the kneeling Mary Temple, showing one fire-crimsoned cheek.

With her ready laughter, which was hearty and whole-souled without a suggestion of boisterousness, Mrs. Charmian Reemy seated herself. Then Andy and Doctor Shonto found seats one on either side of her.

"This is certainly a refreshing experience, Mrs. Reemy," were the younger man's first words since acknowledging his introduction to her.

"I'm glad you think so," she replied. "I dearly love to make life refreshing for folks. For myself as well. I thought it would be refreshing fun to dress to-night, with only Mary Temple and me 'way out here in the woods. It was just a freakish whim of mine. I get 'em frequently. Don't I, Mary Temple?"

The firelight showed red through one of Mary Temple's thin ears as she half turned her head, doubtless to administer a reproof, and executed "eyes front" again when she changed her mind.

"I had no idea at the time, though, that two distressed gentlemen were to come to my party and admire me and my table decorations."

She swept a white arm in the direction of a table at one side of the large room, on which were a spotless cloth, china and silver, and an earth-sweet centerpiece of ferns and California holly berries.

"Now I'll tell you who I am, so that you will be better able to celebrate properly with me—and then for the glands. I'm dying to learn all about glands. Could you rejuvenate me, Doctor Shonto? Now's your chance for that pretty birthday speech!"

"I think," said Shonto, with his grave smile, "that you, Mrs. Reemy, are a far more successful rejuvenator right now than I shall ever be. I've sloughed off five years since entering your door."

"Better! That was extremely well done. And now let's get down to business:

"I am Charmian Reemy, aged twenty-two to-day. I was born in San Francisco, and live there now. When I was seventeen I was married to Walter J. Reemy, a mining man from Alaska. To be absolutely frank, that marriage was the result of a plot by my father and mother to marry me off to a wealthy man. And I was too young and pliable to put up a decent fight.

"I went to Alaska with my husband, where we lived two years. He was killed in a gambling game, and his will left everything to me. I sold out his Alaska mining property and returned to the United States, where I lived with my parents in San Francisco until both were taken away in the recent flu epidemic.

"Since then I have been alone except for Mary Temple, who was with me in Alaska. She had returned to San Francisco with me after Walter's death. So when I was left entirely alone again I hunted her up, and she has been my companion and housekeeper ever since.

"When I was little I was what is generally called a misunderstood child. Whether that was true or not I can't say, but I know that, almost from my earliest remembrance, my home life was unpleasant. My parents were plodders in the footsteps of Tradition. At an early age I showed radical tendencies.

"I am a radical to-day. I am intolerant of all the intolerance of this generation of false prophets. I come up here to forget man's stupidity. And I call my retreat in the big-timber country The Throne of Tolerance. Wait until tomorrow morning. Then, if you can look from those west windows and be intolerant of anything or anybody, you don't belong to my clan.

"I make pilgrimage to El Trono de Tolerancia whenever I begin to choke up down in San Francisco. Mary Temple and I live simply up here in the woods until the suffocation passes, then we return to the city—and boredom. I learned to love the outdoors up in Alaska. And sometime I'm going on a great adventure. I'm going to some far-off place where man never before has set his foot. And maybe I shan't come back.

"That's about all there is to be told about me. Except that I never intend to marry again. Oh, yes!—and I always call Mary Temple Mary Temple. If I were to call her Mary it would sound disrespectful from one so much younger than she is. If I called her Miss Temple it would sound stiff and throw a wet blanket over our comradeship. And I'm too human, and I hope too genuine, to ape high society and call her Temple. So she's Mary Temple to me, and everything seems to move smoothly. Now I'm through—positively through. Now tell me about the glands, Doctor Shonto."

Shonto was smiling in quiet amusement. He could not quite make out this girl. Shonto was very much a radical himself, and he believed that she knew it. But he considered her too young to hold such a pessimistic outlook on life as she had hinted at. That she was ready to worship him because of his reputation as a specialist in gland secretions seemed apparent. The doctor had been fawned upon by many women intellectually inclined, and they had nauseated him immeasurably. He admired Charmian Reemy for her physical charm, her vivacity, and her good-fellowship; but he was experienced and therefore wary.

But he was saved for the present from committing himself by Mary Temple, who had completed her ministrations over the Dutch oven, and had carried the result to the table.

"Dinner's ready," she announced unceremoniously.

Whereupon Charmian rose and seated her guests.

Dr. Shonto was not a little puzzled at the behaviour of his friend. Andy Jerome had spoken to Mrs. Reemy but once since their entrance into her home, aside from muttering her name when the doctor had introduced him.

It was true that their hostess had done most of the talking herself, but Shonto had managed to get in a word edgewise now and then. While Andy had showed little or no inclination to talk at all.

For the most part he had sat and almost stared at her, as if never before had he seen a beautiful girl in an evening gown. The doctor knew that this was far from the case, and that Andy ordinarily was quick to respond to pretty women. He usually could hold his own with them, too. But it seemed that Charmian Reemy had fairly swept him off his feet. Shonto felt a slight twinge of regret. He found that he himself was rather impressed by this frank, free-spoken girl of the woods and the cities.

Mary Temple occupied the foot of the table, where she sat stiffly and with an austere mien, and attended to the greater part of the serving. They were no more than seated when Charmian Reemy again began begging the gland specialist to initiate her into the mysteries of his witchcraft. But Shonto, seeking an avenue of escape, hit upon a topic that at once changed her thoughts into another, though no less interesting, channel.

"You say, Mrs. Reemy," he began, "that you are contemplating going off for a big adventure some day. If you haven't anything definite in mind, I'd like to offer a suggestion. How would you like to make an attempt to explore a lost valley—a forgotten valley—in reality, an undiscovered valley?"

"What?" Her dark eyes were sparkling.

"Just that. Andy and I heard about it the other day. And on the way to this undiscovered valley you may hunt for opals. Of course, a fellow may hunt for opals anywhere he chooses. But in this case he may do so with reasonable hopes of success."

"Do you mean that, Doctor Shonto?"

"Absolutely. But I have only the story of a couple of prospectors, one of whom has been an old-time opal miner in Australia. They are both intelligent men, and their story rang true."

"Please let's hear all about it!" begged Charmian. "An undiscovered valley! How can it be undiscovered when these prospectors know about it? And opals! You've lured me away from glands for the present, Doctor. Give us the yarn!"

CHAPTER III
THE PROSPECTOR'S STORY

"WELL," began Dr. Shonto reflectively, "Andy and I were in our camp on the North Fork of the Lizard, about two and a half miles from Lovejoy's place. Two men came along with pack burros, bound up into the Catfish Country—if you know where that is."

Charmian nodded eagerly.

"They stopped, and as lunch was about ready we invited them to eat with us.

"They called themselves Smith Morley and Omar Leach. They are both middle-aged men and seem to have had a great deal of experience at prospecting.

"Well, Andy and I are old-time ramblers ourselves. We spend a great deal of time together in the outlands, mostly just loafing around and enjoying camp life and the scenery. We were able to talk with the pair about many things of interest to both factions. One thing led to another, and finally Smith Morley mentioned that he had hunted for opals with a camel train in Australia. We at once became interested and asked him all about the life. It is vastly entertaining, from his account.

"Then he told us of the California opals, but when Andy asked if he ever found any in this state he grew reticent. Finally, however, when he learned that both of us were men of some means, he told us about certain opal claims that he and his partner had filed on this year, and which they would be obliged to lose because they were financially unable to get into the country and do their assessment work.

"They offered to sell the claims to us, and to take us to them and establish us if we would defray the expenses. Morley showed us one of the handsomest opals I have ever seen. Its fire was simply wonderful—I'd never before seen anything to equal it.

"We weren't greatly interested, however, until they mentioned the undiscovered valley. While Andy has nothing much to occupy his time, I have my investigations to carry on and a great deal of laboratory work, though I am not practising medicine regularly. Anyway, we didn't want to go into the opal-mining game. But, as I said, the undiscovered valley enticed us, and we wanted to know all about it.

"The opal claims are on the desert in what is called the Shinbone Country. It is very difficult to get to them, and the soft, deep sand makes automobiles a failure. One must use horses and pack burros, and at best the water supply is dangerously short. However, the undiscovered valley is something like thirty miles beyond the desert, in the mountains, at an elevation of perhaps eight thousand feet.

"From the description they gave us, those who know of its existence say that it is about thirteen miles long by seven or eight miles in width. It is surrounded by high peaks upon which the snow lies for almost the entire year. These peaks are said to be straight up and down, to use Morley's phrase, and heavily timbered up to the snow-line. The valley is therefore like the crater of an extinct volcano, and many claim that it is just that. To reach the timbered section, one must cross miles and miles of country covered with the densest chaparral. He must either cut his way through it with a knife and an ax or crawl on all fours. This stretch is waterless, and exposed to the sunny side of steep mountains, where the heat beats down unmercifully.

"But assuming that a fellow gets through this chaparral country, he has yet to scale those grim peaks which Morley calls straight up and down. And if he reaches the summit, he then will be obliged to get down into the valley, perhaps several thousand feet in depth.

"The valley was discovered some years ago by a forest ranger. He had climbed to a high peak about sixteen miles distant from it, and assumed that, even then, he was on ground where no man of to-day, at least, had ever stood before. He suffered a great deal on that trip, but determination kept up his courage and he finally reached the goal for which he had set out. And from the summit of that peak he glimpsed the unexplored valley.

"It seems strange that, in this day and age, such a valley could remain unknown. But such seems to be the case. Andy and I have found in our travels over the state that there are vast stretches of forest land where a white man has probably never set his foot. But in almost every case, there was nothing to draw him. This instance is different.

"Fortunately the ranger had a telescope with him, and was able to see a portion of the valley between two of the peaks that surround it. He circulated the report that the valley is wooded, and that a fair-sized river flows down the centre of it. He saw great quantities of meadow land, and on it animals were grazing, but he could not determine what they were. Altogether the valley presented a pleasing outlook, and he made up his mind to explore it.

"He made many trips, alone and with friends, which occupied months. They strove to get at that valley from every angle, and one man lost his life in the attempt. Finally they were obliged to give it up, though they estimated that they had approached to within three miles of their goal. So throughout the Shinbone Country the undiscovered valley is well known to be in existence, but that's the end of it. The country is thinly populated, of course, and the people who live there mind their own business pretty well and are completely out of touch with the outside world. And thus it transpires that the unexplored valley is not generally known to be in existence.

"One of the most remarkable features concerning it is the river that flows through it. All rivers in this country flow in a general westerly direction, of course, toward the Pacific Ocean. Not so the river that flows through the undiscovered valley. It runs due east, according to the ranger, though that may mean much or nothing at all, for it may change to a westward course farther on.

"But the question is, where does it come out of the valley? All of the rivers and streams in that section are known and named. No one can account for a river without a name, flowing toward the coast on the west side of the range. But farther back in the mountains, estimated at about ten miles from the peaks that surround the undiscovered valley, there is what is known as a lost river. In fact, it is called Lost River.

"The source of Lost River is known. It rises from springs high up in the range, and is fed by other springs as it flows westward and gathers width. Then, about ten miles from the high peaks, it vanishes—is swallowed up by the earth in a mountain meadow. It is not just soaked up by the ground, but plunges into a cave in the side of a hill. And, so far as anybody knows, that is the end of it.

"Of course, it is assumed that this river runs underground from that point and eventually reaches the undiscovered valley, where it rises again and flows serenely across the valley—quite a large stream, it seems—and then vanishes once more. And for the remainder of its course to the sea, it may be any one of the known rivers in the Shinbone Country. It probably would not pop up out of the ground in the lowlands so abruptly as it plunges into the cave in the high altitudes. It may rise again as springs—seep up from the soil in a natural way. Or its waters may separate during their underground journey after leaving the unexplored valley, and they may form two or more streams in the lowlands.

"So that's about all there is to be said about the undiscovered valley—or perhaps the unexplored valley would be more proper—and the river that loses itself in the ground. Andy and I grew quite excited over it, but when we tried to pump Morley and Leach to find out the location of the Shinbone Country they refused to come across. Shinbone is a local name, it seems, and few besides the people who live there know it as such. We don't even know what county it is in. Leach and Morley, however, promised to tell us all about it and to take us to it, provided we would interest ourselves in their opal claims. So, as we didn't care to do that, we let the matter slide."

Charmian Reemy had forgotten her dinner and was resting her bare elbows on the table, nesting her chin in her hands. Her dark eyes were fixed on Inman Shonto. And Andy's eyes were fixed on her.

"Where," she asked in a low voice, "are Morley and Leach now?"

"Still on their way to the Catfish Country, I suppose," Shonto replied.

"When was it that they were in your camp?"

"Day before yesterday, about noon—wasn't it, Andy?"

Andy Jerome nodded absently.

"Then they can't have reached the Catfish Country yet," said Charmian. "I'm going after them to-morrow morning. Now, for the first time in my life, I wish I had a car. I could travel in it as far as Jorny Springs, and there I could get a saddle horse and run them down before they get into the wilderness."

"Do you really want to go after opals and the unexplored valley?" asked Andy suddenly.

She turned her dark eyes on him. "I want to more than anything else I've ever wanted to do," she told him.

"Then you can have my car to-morrow morning. And, if you'll let me, I'll go with you after Leach and Morley. And if we find them, and can come to terms with them, I'll—I'll— Well, if we can arrange matters to suit you, I'd like to go with you to the Shinbone Country."

For a short time they gazed into each other's eyes. Andy Jerome's lips were parted, and Shonto noted the quick rise and fall of his breast. Then a slight flush covered Charmian Reemy's cheeks, and her long, dark lashes hid her eyes.

"If we can arrange matters," she said, "I'd—I'd be glad to have you, Mr. Jerome."

Then, with another pang, Dr. Inman Shonto interpreted the strange silence that had existed between these two. It was the result of an odd embarrassment that both had felt since they first clasped hands. It was love at first sight between them, and they were backward and afraid of each other.

The eyes of both now were lowered. Shonto glanced quickly at Mary Temple. Her gaunt face was set in hard lines. She knew, and she disapproved—at least until she knew more about this handsome young man who had invaded their quiet retreat.

And Shonto— Well, Shonto disapproved, too. Shonto was far older than Andy—too old, perhaps, to think of loving a woman of Charmian Reemy's age. But he put all this behind him. If Andy and Charmian were going in search of the unexplored valley, he meant to go along. Several years her senior though he knew himself to be, Shonto believed that he was the man for a woman like Charmian Reemy rather than Andy Jerome. Anyway, he meant to know more about her. It would not do for Andy to win her away from him if she was what he believed her to be. Yes, Shonto would go along, and his life's work could go hang, for all he cared. Until he knew the truth about Charmian Reemy, at any rate.

"We could find it easily, I guess, in an airplane," Andy suggested.

"An airplane!" scoffed the girl. "Not I! I hate airplanes—I hate anything mechanical. I'll find that valley as my forefathers would have found it, or I'll stay away. And I must think up an appropriate name for it. Doctor Shonto seems undecided between 'the undiscovered valley' and 'the unexplored valley.' Neither is romantic enough. I'll think up a name before morning. I like to name things. And I'm going, really—if we can overtake Leach and Morley. Do you approve, Mary Temple?"

"No!" snapped Mary Temple, and passed the venison to Andy with jerky hospitality.

CHAPTER IV
A MEMBER OF THE CLAN

DR. INMAN SHONTO, always an early riser, was the first one stirring at El Trono de Tolerancia the following morning. He left the log house by the door through which he had entered it the night before, and gazed off into the timberland to the east, through which Andy and he had reached the place. He turned and walked around the cabin, and then he realized what Charmian Reemy had meant when she stated that it was next to impossible for one to be intolerant when he looked from her home to the west.

The cabin was set on a gigantic rock that overhung the brow of the mountain. A metal railing had been erected along the edge of the rock to prevent the unwary from plunging down at least forty feet to the rock's massive base. From the base the land sloped off sharply for perhaps half a mile. And beyond that it continued to slope more gently to level wooded stretches below. The great forest over which one looked would have seemed endless were it not for the broad Pacific in the far distance, which began at the end of the mass of green and rolled on to the uttermost ends of the earth.

Never in his life had the nature-loving man seen a more gorgeous picture. It seemed that the very world was laid out for him to gaze upon from that gaunt pinnacle. He stepped to the iron rail, cold and dewy, grasped it in his strong, lean hands, and stood there, bareheaded, reverent.

"Do you feel tolerant of all mankind now, Doctor?" came a low voice at his elbow.

Shonto wheeled about, startled, as if awakened from a dream. Charmian Reemy stood beside him, dressed in a man's flannel shirt, a divided whipcord skirt, and high-laced boots. She had combed her dark brown hair, but had not stopped to do it up. It fell in a cataract, gleaming bronze-gold with the rays of the early-morning sun behind her, almost to her knees. She was smiling that smile which lifted one corner of her mouth in a whimsical little twist.

"I am tolerant of all mankind," said the doctor seriously. "But now that you have come, I don't know whether to look at you or—that." And he pointed over the mysterious forest to the sea, which seemed to stand upright before him as if painted on a huge canvas.

"Do you think I'm pretty?"

"I know it—you're almost beautiful."

"But that," she said, pointing over the forest, "is not only beautiful but mighty—stupendous. You'd better look at that, Doctor."

"The redwood forests are mighty," he told her, "but they are no more beautiful than the redwood lily that hides in the perpetual shade they cast. One cannot say that the giant redwood tree is more wonderful than the slender lily at its feet. Both are the product of nature's mysterious laboratory. And you are, too."

"Speaking of tolerance," she went on, without comment upon his comparison, "don't you think that we could all be more tolerant of others if we only would look at every one we meet as a distinct product of nature? I mean this: We say, 'Here is a redwood tree. Isn't it magnificent?' Or, 'Here is a redwood lily. Doesn't it smell sweet?' Or, 'Here is a buckthorn bush. Aren't its spines prickly?' We never think of comparing them. We would not say, 'This redwood lily is puny compared with a redwood tree.' Or, 'This buckthorn bush is so prickly. I don't think nearly so much of it as I do of the whitethorn bush, which has beautiful flowers and is soft to the touch.' Wouldn't that sound ridiculous! We accept all things in nature as they are, except man. For man we have set a standard, and he must live up to it or be forever displeasing to us. I wonder if you know what I'm talking about."

"I think I understand you perfectly," replied Shonto. "And I believe that you are entirely right. In fact, my life's work is based on what you have just expressed."

"The glands?" she asked eagerly.

"Yes."

"Won't you please explain? We have lots of time. None of the others are up yet."

Dr. Shonto was tempted. "It is my firm belief," he said, "that man's daily life—all that he does and all that he is—depends almost entirely upon his gland secretions. His height, his attitude toward others, the colour of his complexion, his strength or weakness, his ability or lack of ability—all this, and much more, is controlled by his glands, or their secretions. The glands are collections of cells which make substances that bring about a specific effect on the economy of the body. The microscope proves that every gland is a chemical factory, and the product of these factories is their secretions. For instance, the sweat glands manufacture perspiration, the lachrymal glands manufacture tears.

"The thyroid gland—the most interesting of all—consists of two dark-red masses in the neck, above the windpipe, and near the larynx. A narrow strip of the same tissue connects them. The secretion of the thyroid glands is called thyroxin, and it contains a relatively high per cent of iodine. The more thyroid a person has the faster does he live. An abundance of thyroid causes one to feel, sense, and think more quickly. The less he has the slower will be his mental processes. And the thyroid gland puts iodine into our blood.

"Sea water, you know, contains iodine. And as man was originally a creature of the sea, iodine is necessary to his existence. There is little or no iodine in the food we eat, so, when man became a land animal, Nature gave him the thyroid gland to supply him with this necessary element. In certain parts of the world—in high altitudes and fresh-water regions—the water does not contain enough iodine. In such regions goiter is prevalent.

"To sum up very briefly the workings of the thyroid gland, life is worth while when it is sufficiently active; and when it is not, life is a burden to the unfortunate individual so affected. It is my belief, then, that when we come to know more about the glands we will realize that man is regulated by them. Then we will be more tolerant, won't we?—and seek to rectify the errors rather than condemn promiscuously?

"It would be next to impossible for me to tell you all that has been discovered about the functions of the various glands. There are the thyroids, the pituitary, the adrenals, the pineal, the thymus, the interstitial, the parathyroids, and the pancreas to be dealt with; but for you and me the thyroids are by far the most important. And I regret to say that I am not in a position to go into the matter thoroughly with you at this time."

"But you haven't told me anything!" she expostulated.

He looked at her gravely. "I really do not feel free to discuss the subject," he said. "I hope you'll pardon me."

Her dark eyes showed a trace of embarrassment as she turned them upon his face. "I'm sorry," she said. "I didn't mean to intrude. I guess it was stupid of me to ask a specialist to disclose his secrets to me."

"It's not that," he told her. "But there is a reason why I must refrain from discussing this subject with you just now. Perhaps at some later date I shall find it possible to go into the matter more fully. And you don't need to apologize. I have no professional secrets. But, as I said, for a rather strange reason, I must not be the one to initiate you into the mysteries of the gland secretions, and what science has accomplished in the way of treating patients who are lacking in these secretions. I'm extremely sorry, Mrs. Reemy, for I must confess that, ordinarily, I like to talk about my work."

She continued to gaze at him, completely mystified; then she showed her good breeding by dropping the subject entirely.

"I have thought up a name for the undiscovered valley," she announced.

"Good! Let's have it."

"The Valley of Arcana."

Dr. Shonto lifted his scanty eyebrows. "Arcana," he repeated. "That sounds familiar. Let me paw through my vocabulary.... I've got it. 'Arcanum' is the singular, isn't it? And it means something hidden from ordinary men. In medicine it means a great secret remedy—a panacea. But you use it in the first sense—a mystery. Or in the plural, 'arcana'—mysteries. The Valley of Mysteries. Good! A dandy!"

"Give Webster the credit," she said demurely. "I stumbled upon the word by accident last night, browsing through the dictionary in search of something new. I'm surprised, and a little piqued, that you knew the meaning. I thought I was springing something on you."

She turned her head quickly as she spoke, and once more the doctor saw the pink creep into her cheeks.

"Mr. Jerome is up," she said, "and is coming around the house to find us. Don't say anything. I mean, don't call his attention to that." She pointed over the glistening forest to the sea once more. "I want to see how he reacts to it when he steps up here and finds it suddenly stretched out before him."

"I'd like to ask you a question," the doctor declared quickly. "Do you really intend to go to the Shinbone Country?"

"Why, certainly—if everything turns out all right."

"When?"

"Right away."

"But it is rather late in the season for such an undertaking, isn't it? Winter is almost upon us."

"But doesn't the assessment work have to be done on the opal mines immediately in order to hold them?"

"I'd forgotten about that," said Shonto.

And then came Andy's "Good morning," as he stepped to the rail beside Charmian and caught his first glimpse of the stupendous scene below him.

"Lord!" he breathed. "Oh, Lord! Look at that!"

And Charmian Reemy smiled. Andy Jerome had shown himself to be a member of her clan.

CHAPTER V
THE CONFERENCE AT JORNY SPRINGS

IT was seven o'clock in the morning when Andy Jerome set off on Charmian Reemy's gray saddler for his camp. A trail led direct from El Trono de Tolerancia to the county road, and once upon it Andy could not possibly miss the way. He was to leave the horse at Lovejoy's, a wilderness resort, and continue on afoot to camp. There he would get his big touring car and drive back to a point in the county road opposite Charmian's home. She and the doctor were to travel after him afoot and meet him there. And Mary Temple had flatly refused to allow Charmian to "go traipsin' off with a couple o' strange men the Lord knew where," so she had truculently constituted herself one of the party.

Andy met the trio about noon. Dr. Shonto took the seat in the tonneau with the stern-faced Mary Temple, and Charmian rode in front with Andy. The handsome big car purred along through the solemn redwoods, following the level valley which paralleled the coast, with a range of wooded mountains between. Gray squirrels scurried across the narrow road, to scamper up lofty trees and bark at them mockingly. The streams that they crossed were riotous and roared about the huge boulders in their courses. The sun scarcely penetrated the dark avenues of the forest. Huckleberry bushes lined the road, the berries ripe and coloured like grapes.

They estimated that the prospectors would not make over twenty miles a day with their slow-moving burros, and maybe less. It was about fifty miles from the North Fork of the Lizard to the outskirts of the Catfish Country; so, as they were virtually two days and a half behind the men, Andy pushed the big car at every opportunity. But the road was so narrow, and there were so many abrupt turns in it, made necessary by gigantic trees, that the driver averaged little better than fifteen miles an hour.

But they reached Jorny Springs, at the gateway to the Catfish Country, before four o'clock that afternoon. And there, to their great satisfaction, they found the prospectors in camp. One of the burros had gone lame on them, and they were resting the little animal before beginning the rough journey into the wilds that lay before them.

Jorny Springs was a backwoods resort conducted by an old man and his wife. They bottled the effervescent water that bubbled up in a dozen places from the ground, and shipped it to San Francisco, where it was known in cafes and soft-drink establishments as Jorny Water. Every house in that country was, on occasion, a hotel and summer resort, and such places were known as stations.

Smith Morley and Omar Leach were camped under the big trees by one of the springs. Shonto went over and talked with them a little, while Charmian and Andy ordered lunch at the house. The doctor returned to them before lunch was ready and made his report of the preliminary conference.

"They are willing enough to drop their present prospecting project right now," he began. "They have gold claims up in the Catfish Country, but their importance is more or less problematical. However, they had enough capital to make this trip, they say, but could not rake up enough for the Shinbone expedition. So they will be only too glad to deal with us."

"What do they want?" asked Charmian.

"I didn't go into that with them," replied Shonto. "But I imagine they prefer to sell the claims outright rather than to take in partners. If you'll accept my advice, Mrs. Reemy, you'll be mighty careful what kind of a deal you make with these boys. They may be all right, and their claims may be all that they say, but, somehow or other, I don't just fancy their looks."

"The one you pointed out to me as Morley," said Charmian, "is a delightful looking villain. I like to deal with villains. That is, I think I should. I've never had an opportunity. I do hope they try to put something over on us."

Shonto and Andy laughed heartily at this, but the austere Mary Temple tightened her thin lips and glared at the young widow.

"Mary Temple refuses to let me have any fun in life," said Charmian. "She doesn't understand my romantic and adventuresome nature in the least. She wants everything to move along smoothly. Well, everything has always moved entirely too smoothly to suit me. I want a few obstacles set in my path. I want to have things happen to me. I want to live!"

After lunch the quartette approached the prospectors. Dr. Shonto introduced Charmian and Mary Temple, and all found seats on stones or logs or filled pack-bags.

Charmian was eying the two men closely.

Smith Morley was dark and tall, and his features were fine except for the black eyes, which were set too close together. Omar Leach was older and heavier, with a sprinkling of grey in his hair. His face was full and inclined to be red. He looked to be a powerful man.

When they spoke Charmian was surprised. Both used good, everyday English, and Morley's account of his opal seeking in Australia was intensely interesting and fired her imagination. They talked for half an hour before Morley spoke of the matter that had brought them together. And when he did so he made the plain statement that the opal claims in the Shinbone

Country were for sale, on a cash basis, and that he and Leach would take the others to them, prove their value, and do anything in reason to establish them.

"And how much do you ask for the claims?" asked the girl.

"Fifty thousand dollars," was Morley's prompt reply.

Before she could express surprise at the amount, or make any comment whatever, Smith Morley reached into an inner pocket of his canvas coat and took out a wad of tissue paper. He deliberately unfolded it, and dropped seven large opals into the girl's hand.

"Look 'em over," he invited. "They all came from our claims. And there are plenty more like them to be found."

"They're beautiful," admitted Charmian, turning a stone this way and that so that it might catch the light filtering down through the treetops. "But I can't understand why, if you can find gems like these, it doesn't pay you to work the claims and make them defray their own expenses."

"We could do it if we were there," put in Omar Leach. "But we're practically broke, and it's a long, expensive trip to the Shinbone Country."

"Then why don't you sell these?" she asked, rattling the opals in her hand.

"We've kept them to show prospective buyers," explained Morley. "We tried all summer to interest somebody, and that's one reason why we're so short of funds. Showing the gems and trying to induce somebody to take hold caused us to lose lots of time, when we ought to have been working for our winter's grubstake. When we saw that our efforts were a failure, we worked a little and got together a small grubstake for this trip into the Catfish Country. Our placer claims up in there are pretty good, and we can sometimes pan out as high as twenty-five dollars a day. It's seldom that we run less than ten dollars. So we thought we could get up there and pan enough to get us down into the Shinbone Country before winter set in. Then we could rush things and finish our assessment work before the end of the year. But if a person had money, Mrs. Reemy, he could get down there at once and hire half a dozen men to finish the work in short order. Then he could sit pretty until spring, provided he didn't care to winter it in the Shinbone Country and dig for opals."

"You'll pardon me for what may seem to be an insolent question," said the girl, "but how do I know that you did not bring these opals from Australia?"

Smith Morley laughed and shrugged. "You have every right to look into the matter from every angle," he exonerated her. "We want you to be cautious and investigate thoroughly. That's business, Mrs. Reemy. Of course we can't prove to you now that those stones didn't come from Australia, or that they did come from our claims. But we can show you when you reach the Shinbone Country."

"When can you start?"

"Just as soon as we can make arrangements with somebody to take care of our outfit, Mrs. Reemy. We can put the burros on pasture here at Jorny Springs, I guess, and cache the outfit. Unless it would be more advisable to take the outfit along. I have an idea we'll be ready to hit the trail to-morrow."

"And how do we go?"

"Well, by train, if you prefer. Or if we had a couple of machines like the one you drove here in—"

"We have two," put in Dr. Shonto briefly.

Both Charmian and Andy Jerome glanced at him curiously.

"Why, you're not going along, are you, Doctor?" asked the girl.

"If I'm welcome, I am," he stated.

"Why, of course you're welcome!" cried Andy. "But—but I'm surprised, Doctor."

"Don't let it affect you too seriously, Andy," said Shonto, with his quiet smile. "Don't you suppose that I am interested in a project like this one?"

"But you weren't the other day," his friend pointed out.

"The other day is not to-day," said the doctor. "In other words, I've changed my mind. I'll be frank. I wouldn't consider going at all if Mrs. Reemy weren't taking the matter up. I think she'll need my mature judgment in many things; and I mean to go along—if she wants me to—and give her the benefit of it."

"Nothing would delight me more than to have you go, Doctor," Charmian said quickly. "But can you spare the time?"

"I can," he replied. "I haven't had a real vacation in the past ten years. And it strikes me that a fellow might run across some new medicinal herbs up in your Valley of Arcana. For all we know, there may be valuable scientific phenomena in that valley that only await discovery. Your valley, Mrs. Reemy, tempts me more than the opal mines. But to find the location of the valley, it seems, we must tackle the mines. So if everything turns out satisfactorily when we get to the Shinbone Country, I'll go partners with you on the opal project."

"Let's make it a triple partnership," Andy suggested.

"That suits me," said Charmian. "To be frank, I hardly wanted to go into the thing alone. This is going to be my life's big adventure—the adventure that I have been planning for and longing for and waiting for for several years. This looks like the big opportunity at last—and I'm going to take a chance."

And here a new voice piped up.

"Charmian Reemy," said Mary Temple, "you are not going down into that hideous country with the hideous name in the company of four strange men."

"Why, old dear," laughed Charmian, "two of them are not strangers at all."

"What two are not, please?"

"Doctor Inman Shonto is known all over the United States and Europe," Charmian pointed out. "And Mr. Jerome is his friend. What better recommendation could one ask for, Mary Temple?"

"There will be four men, and only two women," Mary told her. "And it's— it's all but downright indecent."

"Two women?"

"Certainly. You are one, and I am one."

"Oh, you mean to go, too, then? I thought you would return to San Francisco and wait there for me."

"If you persist in going into that boneyard country, Charmian, I am going with you. And that ends that."

"Well, goodness knows you're welcome, Mary Temple," laughed Charmian. "But I didn't for a minute imagine that you would care to go."

"I don't," snapped Mary Temple. "But that's not saying I'm not going. And there must be two more women in the party."

"Oh, Mary Temple! What a prig you are! Do you want to pair us off?"

"Common decency demands that there be as many women as there are men," declared Mary.

"We might take my wife along," Smith Morley put in. "She's in Los Angeles now. She could meet us at ———. Well, I'll arrange that. But Leach hasn't a wife—yet. Wouldn't three women do, Miss Temple? Another person would make the two machines pretty full, you know. We'll have a world of baggage to pile in the tonneaus and lash on the running-boards."

"What is your wife like?" demanded Mary Temple unfeelingly.

"Why, Mary Temple! What an impertinent question!" cried Charmian.

"Impertinent or not," barked Mary, "I want to know what his wife is like before I give my consent."

Morley only laughed and showed no resentment. "Why, she's a pretty good old girl," he told her. "She's a good housewife, not bad looking, a good dresser when I'm in luck, and pretty rough and ready when it comes to camp life in the wilderness. You'll like her, I think."

"Have you any children?" demanded Mary.

"No."

Mary sighed and clasped her veiny hands. "Well," she declared, "I'd feel safer if you had a child to take along—preferably a little girl of seven or eight. The child, perhaps, would restrain you if you had anything evil in your mind."

"Mary Temple, I'm ashamed of you!" Charmian half laughed, and the colour flooded her face.

"I'm only looking out for your interests, my dear," said Mary. "If I didn't, who would? I distrust men on general principles, as you know very well. But if you're determined to go, Charmian, we can at least travel to where we are to meet Mrs. Morley. Then if she suits me, we'll go on. If not, we'll come back."

"You're a regular tyrant, Mary Temple!" pouted Charmian.

"I know it," Mary retorted. "But I get results."

CHAPTER VI
SECOND SIGHT

BECAUSE Mary Temple was afraid to ride over the narrow curving road after dark, the four prospective adventurers remained at Jorny Springs all night. Before going to bed Charmian, coached by the doctor, made arrangements with Leach and Morley to go to San Francisco and sign certain papers to show good faith, which papers would be drawn up by the young widow's attorney. When this matter had been settled, they were to drive together to the Shinbone Country—wherever that was—and make a thorough investigation of the properties.

Both Leach and Morley had protested against entering into a written agreement. They offered to produce references which ought to satisfy the most suspicious, but Dr. Shonto remained firm. Finally, seeing no way around the obstacle, they consented, but declared that they begrudged the time that would be taken up by the trip to San Francisco.

After the plain, old-fashioned dinner served by the owners of Jorny Springs, Charmian took a walk through the twilight. Shortly after she left the house Andy Jerome set off in the opposite direction, stating that he too would like a stroll. But when the great trees hid him from the house he made a swift circle back, and soon was on Charmian's trail. He found her leaning over a fence, watching a dozen fat and shockingly muddy pigs in a stake-and-rider corral.

"I see you prefer to choose your own company," he observed, as he rested his arms on the fence beside her. "I hope one more won't constitute a crowd."

"Aren't they funny!" she laughed. "I love pigs and things like that. Cows and chickens and horses and everything. Do you know that I, as the head of the expedition to be, intend to make a hard-and-fast ruling at the very outset? It's this: No one in the party will be permitted to kill any living thing."

"Why, that's a funny idea," he laughed. "If a fellow can't do a little hunting to pass away dull hours, how's he going to amuse himself? And it may be that we'll frequently find ourselves in need of fresh meat."

"I don't care," she said. "I don't approve of the slaughter of the innocents. I used to hunt myself, but I gave it up. I can't bear to take a life. Man can't create, yet in the winking of an eyelid he can and will destroy a life that he can never reproduce. It's the same with a tree. One can cut down a tree in thirty minutes which nature has spent hundreds of years in growing. And man can't replace it. Whenever I hear one of these giant redwoods fall groaning under the ax my heart fairly bleeds."

"But man must live," Andy pointed out.

"I don't know whether he must or not," she said seriously. "He's made a complete botch of existence. Sometimes I wish the entire race were wiped out, so nature could begin all over again. Man is as barbarous to-day as he was a thousand years ago. The only difference is that he has invented new machinery with which to practise his barbarism."

"Why, you're a regular little cynic!" Andy accused.

"Perhaps. I have little patience with mankind, if that's what you mean. The so-called lower animals have my love and sympathy. They haven't made a farce of their lives, as we have. And vivisection—that's what makes me wild! Man, by his own selfish indulgences, by his reckless living, his complete disregard of the laws of nature, has succeeded in shortening his life and depleting his physical vigour. So, in his eagerness to continue the debauch, scared stiff at thought of the yawning precipice just ahead of him, he turns in his cowardly way to the so-called lower animals. He robs these helpless creatures of their health and vitality in order to patch up his poor, miserable, worthless body. Like the five foolish virgins, men say to these wise virgins—these innocents of the earth who have conserved their oil of life—'Give us of your oil, for our lamps are gone out.' Could anything be more cowardly, Mr. Jerome?"

"But aren't the lower animals placed on this earth for the benefit of man?" asked Andy.

"Oh, yes—man imagines everything on earth is put here for him to exploit and ruin! Where are the buffaloes? Where are the beavers? Where are the elks? Where are the bighorns? Were they put here for man to destroy—to wipe almost completely from the face of the earth? When man has learned to step down from his papier-mâché throne of insufferable conceit, he will find that he is only a part of nature's scheme—that every other atom in the universe is as important as he is. Then we can begin to look for the dawn of civilization."

"I'm afraid," said Andy, "that you and Doctor Shonto are not destined to get along very well together."

"Why?"

"Well, it is his business to exploit nature for the rebuilding of man."

"Yes—I know. I tried to draw him out this morning, but he refused to be tempted into a discussion of his work. How long have you known him, Mr. Jerome?"

"Why, almost all my life, it seems. He is an old friend of my father and mother. I can't remember when I didn't know the doctor."

"That seems strange. He is not so much older than you are. How old are you?"

"Twenty-four," Andy replied.

"And I should say the doctor is not much over thirty."

"Thirty-four, I believe."

"Then he was ten years old when you were born. Could you call him a 'friend of your father and mother' when he was ten years old? Did you play with him when you were a boy?"

For a long time Andy Jerome was silent. Then he said slowly:

"I must tell you something about myself. I can recall almost nothing of my childhood before my twelfth birthday. And my earliest recollections are of Doctor Shonto. I remember him as about twenty-two or twenty-three years old. And, to me, he never was younger than that."

"Why, I can't understand you at all!" exclaimed the girl.

"It's very difficult to understand," he said in low tones. "But when I was about eight years old, they tell me, something happened to me. It seems that I got a crack on the noodle while playing and lost my memory. I remained in that condition from the age of eight until I was perhaps between eleven and twelve. It was Doctor Shonto, who had just been graduated from a medical college and was already making a big name for himself, who treated me and brought me out of my coma. But, strange to say, it left me with a weak heart. I have to take treatment for it right along, and the doctor tells me that, if I neglect this treatment, my old condition will come back, or I may suddenly drop dead. For all that, I'm fit as a fiddle and strong as an ox. It seems funny to think that I may bump off at any moment—hard to believe. But nobody ever doubts Doctor Shonto. However, he has assured me again and again that I have nothing whatever to worry about, so long as I take my medicine diligently. I guess I haven't missed a day since he began his treatment."

"Why, how strange!" was Charmian's only comment.

"It is strange—mighty strange. Now and then I get a faint glimmering of something that took place before I was eight years of age, but it's so hazy that it seems like it happened to some one else instead of me. And it seemed that, when I gradually regained my memory, I was being born all over again. I had the mind of a child of two or three, though I was over twelve years old. I remembered nothing of what had been taught me in the private school that they told me I had once attended. I had to begin my schooling at the very bottom again. Lord, how they made me cram! I studied night and day, and seemed eager enough to learn. They tell me that I have caught up because of my perpetual digging—that I now have the mentality of a normal man of my age. And so for the past year I have studied very little, and have been catching up on the physical end. I have lived in the open months at a time, and frequently Doctor Shonto has been with me. He likes it himself, and he likes to be with me. And I can tell you right here and now that I think Doctor Inman Shonto the greatest man alive!"

"I'll bet you do," said Charmian warmly. "But it strikes me as rather strange that you should never call him Doc, since you two are so close."

"I guess I'd never think of calling him that," said Andy reflectively. "No, that wouldn't seem the proper thing to do."

"What do you do when you're at home, Mr. Jerome?"

"Why, I hope to become a lawyer some day," he replied. "You see, I'm still a student. I've studied law a little and mean to take up a regular course next year. But for the present my parents and Doctor Shonto think it best for me to loaf around outdoors."

"I suppose your folks are wealthy," said Charmian in her frank way.

"Yes, they're accounted so. Pop has retired. He was a candy and cracker manufacturer. I'd like to have you meet my mother. She's a peach. You'd like her. She'd like you, too."

"And so your hero is Doctor Inman Shonto," mused Charmian. "I wonder if it would be proper for me to ask you about his work, after he himself has refused to tell me anything?"

"Precious little I can tell you," laughed Andy. "But I'll do my best. If Doctor Shonto has any secrets, they're safe with me because I couldn't explain them if I wanted to. Fire ahead. Doctor Shonto doesn't like to talk about himself. He's entirely too modest."

"I wanted to ask you," said the girl, "if Doctor Shonto is in any way responsible for the horrible things I have read about in the papers lately. Rich men hiring thugs to waylay strong, healthy men, knock them out, and take them to doctors, who operate on them and steal their glands, which are substituted for the worn-out glands of the rich men?"

"Nothing doing!" loyally cried Andy. "Doctor Shonto says the most of that news is nothing but hot air. No, he never uses human glands in his work. He uses sheep glands exclusively. And the animals are killed before he cuts the glands out of them."

"Are you positive?"

"I have only his word for it. But he's a very tender-hearted man—for a surgeon. And he has a magnificent sense of justice. No, not in a thousand years would Doctor Shonto countenance anything like that."

"I'm glad to hear you say so," she sighed. "I think that is simply horrible—ghoulish! But why was it, then, that the doctor refused to tell me anything about his work?"

"Well, he has accomplished wonders, they say. And, as I told you before, he's modest."

"Modesty reaps its reward only in fiction."

"I imagine the doctor is keener after results than rewards," Andy mused. "I'll tell you the little that I have gleaned—mostly about the thyroid gland, which, you know, is in our throats.

"It seems that, if a fellow is shy on thyroid, he's up against it in many ways. He may be slow to learn, clumsy, and may have an unbalanced sense of right and wrong. If he is fed the extract of the thyroid glands of sheep, this can be corrected.

"It is the same with the other glands in our system. Some control one thing, some another. And, according to Doctor Shonto's theory, the time is close at hand when deficient people can be entirely remade by injecting into them, or feeding them, the extract of the gland secretion that they're shy on. This will revolutionize our social system, according to Doctor Shonto. We will know then that mental defectives, criminals, people who are petulant and hard to get along with—in fact, everybody who is in any way not up to normal—are so because of the absence, or the over-supply, of the secretions of certain glands. This science can correct, and the time may come when we will be able to do away with prisons and corrective institutions, and treat our fellowmen instead of mistreating them."

"Heaven speed the day!" said Charmian fervently. "But why, tell me, did Doctor Shonto hesitate about telling me that?"

Andy shrugged his broad shoulders. "*Quien sabe*," he said, "unless his modesty made him reticent. I think he's afraid of being ridiculed as a visionary theorist."

"Doctor Shonto doesn't strike me as a man who would shrink from ridicule, if he thought he was in the right," Charmian declared.

Two days later the six who were interested in the opal project and the Valley of Arcana arrived in San Francisco late in the evening. It was after business hours, so nothing could be done toward drawing up the papers until the following morning. Charmian called up her attorney, briefly outlined the situation, and arranged for a conference at ten the following day. Then she went to her apartments with Mary Temple, while Andy and Dr. Shonto took rooms in the Palace Hotel. Smith Morley sent a telegram to his wife in Los Angeles, after which he and his partner sought a cheap rooming house on Kearny Street. They were to meet the others in the offices of Charmian's lawyer at eleven o'clock next morning.

Charmian Reemy was tired from the long automobile ride from the wilderness, and went early to bed. Shortly after her retirement Mary Temple stepped softly to her bedroom door and listened until convinced that her young charge was sound asleep. Then she put on her ancient fur coat and her surprisingly old-fashioned hat, and noiselessly left the apartment.

The elevator was still running, and she rode in it to the ground floor, where she slipped out into a cold, foggy night. At the corner she took a streetcar and rode to a point in the city directly opposite Golden Gate Park. Here she left the car, walked three blocks, and rang the bell of a three-story flat.

Presently the door automatically swung open, and she entered a warm, carpeted hall. She briskly ascended a long flight of stairs, at the top of which a large woman in a blue-silk kimono awaited her.

"Oh, it's you, is it, dearie?" greeted the woman. "I thought you were in the country."

"We came back this evening, Madame Destrehan," said Mary, reaching the large woman's side and extending her hand. "And I came direct to you. I'm in trouble again. That little minx has a new wild scheme in her head. I can't talk her out of it. But I'm afraid. I just know there's something wrong."

"Come in and tell me all about it," offered Madame Destrehan. "I know I can help you. I—I—" She placed a fat, white, bejewelled hand to her forehead and brushed across it. "I see something now."

They entered the medium's apartment. Both seated themselves, and Mary Temple poured out the story of the two strangers who had invaded El Trono de Tolerancia, and of the opal claims and the Valley of Arcana. Madame Destrehan listened with both eyes closed. She sat immovable after Mary's cracked voice ceased, her eyelids still lowered.

Then she began waving her plump hands slowly this way and that. She did not open her eyes, but she mumbled something which Mary could not interpret. Then suddenly she began speaking in a low, awed tone.

"I see that valley," said the seventh daughter of a seventh daughter. "It's beautiful, but death stalks across it from end to end. And I see— Oh, horrors! I see an ugly face. The face of a man. It is bluish, and the eyes are popping from the head. The eyes are glazed, and his thick, blue tongue hangs out like the tongue of a tired dog. The man's hair is dishevelled and long. A matted beard covers his face. His eyes stare, then gleam with ferocity. His skin is withered and yellow, and his finger nails are long. He grits his teeth and babbles like a madman. And—oh, horrors! He is leaning over Mrs. Reemy, and his crooked fingers are drawing nearer and nearer to her white throat!"

CHAPTER VII
LOT'S WIFE AND SHIRTTAIL HENRY

THE papers had been signed. Andy Jerome and Dr. Inman Shonto had wired to Los Angeles to explain that they probably would not be home for a month. Smith Morley's wife had arrived in San Francisco, since the adventurers' trip to the city had necessitated a change in their route to the Shinbone Country. Several days were spent in outfitting the expedition. And just a week after Dr. Shonto had told Charmian Reemy of the prospectors they set off early in the morning, with Charmian, Andy, and Mr. and Mrs. Morley in the leading car.

Two days later, having driven leisurely and stopped at hotels en route, they negotiated a steep, wooded pass and saw the yellow desert stretched out before them, three thousand feet above the sea. Across it continued the road, straight as a carpenter's chalk-line, until it contracted to a pinpoint in the hazy distance and disappeared with the curvature of the earth.

The big cars wallowed into the sandy ruts and continued on. Weird growths were on either side of the road—great flat-palmed cacti, whispering yucca palms, scattering greasewood bushes. The wind was strong, and the sand was driven into the travellers' faces in waves. Now and then the cars crossed dry lakes, which, before they reached them, had looked deceptively wet. These were smooth, like hardened plaster of Paris, except that now and then the mud, in drying, had cracked and peeled, leaving a sea of shards that extended for many miles. Nothing at all grew on the dark surface of these dry lakes.

In the dim distance a hazy line of calico buttes appeared after an hour of fast travel over the desert. As the machines neared them a long line of mountains showed behind the buttes, and the uninitiated of the party were told that between the buttes and the range of wooded mountains lay another stretch of desert as barren as the one they then were crossing. The buttes marked the beginning of the Shinbone Country, which extended into the higher altitudes. In the buttes were the opal claims.

They came to an oasis, green with alfalfa. Here for forty years a family had lived because of the artesian water that spurted up from the level land. The cottonwood trees, though they had shed their leaves for the coming winter, looked inviting to the sand-blistered pilgrims. The place was called Diamond H Ranch, and the owner herded his cattle on the desert during winter months, when bunchgrass grew, and drove them to the distant mountains for the summer grazing.

Not until they reached the ranch did Smith Morley inform his prospective buyers that here their journey by automobile would end. There was a huge stable, and in it there was plenty of room to store the cars. Also, Morley told them, they would meet with no difficulty in buying or hiring saddle horses and pack animals from the ranchman. Furthermore, he conducted a tiny store in connection with his ranch, and if it should become necessary to do so, they could return to the ranch at any time and purchase such staple articles of food as might be needed.

Roger Furlong was the rancher's name. He and his family made the guests welcome and treated them hospitably. The afternoon was spent in the selection of saddle stock, and the rancher's boy was sent scouring the desert for a herd of burros, which were at large and living off the sage. It was late in the afternoon before the herd was rounded up and driven in to the corrals. Here Furlong picked out twelve animals that were old-time packers. The outfit's supplies and paraphernalia were transferred from the tonneaus and running-boards of the machines to the pack-bags. When darkness came everything was ready for an early start for the calico buttes the following morning.

All of which caused Mary Temple to register a look of high disapproval.

Mary had roughed it considerably in Alaska, so the trip in the saddle had no terrors for her. Neither did she shrink from their proposed sojourn in a wild, waterless, and unfriendly country. But she was amazed and resentful over the whole proceedings.

In San Francisco, while they were outfitting, she had done her utmost to dissuade Charmian from continuing her erratic undertaking. But that young lady had a mind of her own and was not to be led astray from her life's great adventure. Every plan for preventing her from going having failed, Mary had recourse to a recital of what Madame Destrehan's second sight had revealed to her. At this Charmian had scoffed disdainfully and laughed hilariously, for Charmian was well aware that Mary often consulted people who claimed to have occult powers. So Mary perforce carried out her original intention and made one of the party, for only death could separate her from Charmian Reemy. But as preparations for the final lap of their journey went forward she continued to glare her displeasure and to shake her greying head with misgivings.

They left Diamond H Ranch at sunup next morning, driving the laden burros ahead of them. Their course took them at right angles to the road over which they had reached the oasis, and extended in a northeasterly direction through the trackless sage and greasewood.

The sand grew heavier as they progressed. The wind came up and drove clouds of it into their faces, sometimes with stinging force. Laden with alkali as it was, their lips and eyelids soon began to swell, and their throats grew parched. They drank heavily of the water in the desert bags on the burros' backs, for Morley assured the party that there would probably be sufficient water near the claims at that time of year. There was an intermittent spring in the buttes, he explained, that went dry during the hot months through evaporation. But with the approach of winter, even though no rain had fallen, the water rose again in the spring because the evaporation was lessened by the coolness in the air.

They camped at noon, halfway to the buttes. The morning had been cool and bracing, and the temperature of the noontide was moderate. Morley informed the newcomers that in less than a month the weather would be cool enough to suit any of them, and that snow, even, might sweep down from the mountains and lie on the ground for several hours.

It was a long, hard trip, for none of them, with the exception of the young widow, had been in the saddle to any great extent for many months. Charmian rode just behind the waddling burros, with Andy at her side. Shonto rode beside Mary Temple, who for the most part made an uncommunicative companion. The prospectors rode with Morley's wife in the rear, and the trio had very little to say to the others.

Dr. Shonto watched Andy and Charmian and could not help but admire them. Physically they were well suited to each other, and both were young and handsome. Since their first meeting Shonto had taken note of the gradual drawing together of the two. He realized that, on the surface of things, this was as it should be. They were equals socially and intellectually, and few there were who would not have called it a fine match.

Still, Dr. Shonto knew in his heart that he could not allow this thing to go on and culminate in the age-old life partnership between man and woman. He sincerely believed that he himself was the man for Charmian Reemy. Never before had he met a woman who appealed to him as she did, both physically and mentally. Despite the difference in their ages, he felt that he, rather than Andy, was the one to satisfy her and round out her life to a point as near completeness as humanity can achieve. She was far older than Andy mentally. Andy was only a strong, handsome boy. He—the doctor—was a man of experience, of achievement, of broad ideals. But all that aside, Dr. Shonto knew that he was falling in love with Charmian, and that, if necessary, he would sacrifice Andy's friendship to win her. For love is primitive; and when a man of the doctor's age and experience falls in love for the first time he makes a rival that will brook no interference. In shorter phraseology, the doctor wanted this girl—and he meant to have her.

As the long evening shadows crawled over the yucca- and cactus-studded wastes the party entered the buttes. Here they found relief from the monotonous desolation they had left, for huge rocks squatted on either side of their course, and the yuccas were larger and seemed more friendly. The buttes themselves showed a variety to which the level land could not lay claim, and here and there was a juniper tree, alone and unwatered, but displaying a greenery that made it in a way companionable.

Darkness had overtaken them when Smith Morley called a halt. They were far within the chain of buttes, in an enfilade with walls of stone towering high above them on either side. They had reached the spring, and, after an examination of it, the prospector made the welcome announcement that there was considerable water in the natural stone basin beneath the drip. For some time, however, the water supply would be short, and it would possibly prove necessary to take the saddle horses into the mountains, the foothills of which were about five miles distant, and leave them there in a certain well-watered meadow of which the opal miners knew. The burros, camel-like, could live on very little water; and the spring perhaps would drip enough for them and the domestic use of the party. The claims were two miles farther on, in the direction of the mountains.

They pitched camp at once. Leach and Mrs. Morley went on a search for petrified yucca with which to build a fire. The others unpacked the burros, hobbled the horses, and pitched the tents.

Mary Temple, because of her superior culinary knowledge—which no one disputed—constituted herself camp cook; and the first thing she had not condemned since leaving El Trono de Tolerancia was the excellent fire that the petrified yucca made. Her appetizing supper was ready before the last tent had been pitched, and they all gathered around it under the cold desert stars and ate as enjoyably as their cracked and swollen lips would permit.

All were excessively weary, and, though the meal revived their spirits in a measure, no one would have been averse to seeking his roll of blankets at an early hour. This, however, was forestalled by the sound of a voice that came suddenly from the night about them—a strange, cracked voice that startled them.

"Hello!" it said. "I hope and trust ye ain't used up all the water in the spring, 'cause I ain't had a drop since noon, an' Lot's Wife ain't had none since yistiddy mornin'."

Omar Leach, who was reclining on one elbow placidly smoking a short briar pipe, flipped himself to a sitting posture and stared at Morley. Morley's face twitched, and his close-set eyes seemed to narrow perceptibly as he gazed back at his partner.

Then Leach gave himself another flip and was on his feet. "Get outa here!" he bawled. "Go on home, and you'll find plenty of water. We're tired and want to go to bed and can't be bothered with you."

"Oh, it's you, is it, Omar?" called the voice. "An' ye'd send me on to the mountains without a drink, would ye? It's like ye, by gum! Well, I'm comin' in for water for me an' Lot's Wife. Maybe the rest o' yer gang ain't so all-fired selfish. C'm'ere, ye pillar o' salt! Wait a min-ut, can't ye!"

This last apparently was addressed to Lot's Wife, who, when she dashed into camp and buried her muzzle in the spring basin, proved to be a slant-eared, knock-kneed female burro as shaggy as the trunk of a shell-bark hickory. After her plodded a man, who had lost his hold on her lead-rope.

Smith Morley darted toward the burro and gave her a kick in the belly that brought a grunt of pain from her. He drew back his leg for another, but found himself facing Charmian Reemy's flashing eyes.

"You kick that burro again," she said, "and I start for home to-morrow morning. So that's the kind of man you are, is it? You would keep a fellow traveller in this forsaken land and his burro from drinking water, would you? Well, Mr. Morley, I don't know whether it is safe to trust in a business deal a man who has such selfishness in his heart as you have shown. I may decide to go back anyway."

Smith Morley looked foolish and embarrassed.

"But you don't understand, Mrs. Reemy," he defended himself. "This water is mighty precious. We'll have to let it drip twelve hours to get enough for ourselves and the pack animals for a day; and I can see right now that the horses will have to go to the mountains in the morning. And this fellow here—I know him well. He's the recognized nuisance of the Shinbone Country. A burro can go for days without water—they're like a camel, Mrs. Reemy. And this old desert rat can do it, too. He's less than ten miles from his home. Why don't he go there for his water? We were here first. It's first come first served in the Shinbone Country, when it comes to water."

"Ten miles is a long trip when one hasn't had a drink in about seven hours," said Charmian. Then she wheeled upon the comical figure that had followed the burro into camp.

"Your burro shall have all the water she needs," she promised him. "And you may fill up your bags, if you have any. I'm Mrs. Charmian Reemy, of San Francisco, and this lady is my companion, Miss Mary Temple. These two gentlemen are Doctor Shonto and Mr. Jerome, of Los Angeles. You know the others, it seems. We're here to investigate their opal claims."

The man was tall, and his bronzed face was covered with ragged brown whiskers. His eyes were large and blue and innocent-looking. His clothes were far too large for him, enormous though his body was. Quaintness stood out all over him.

"I'm reg'lar glad to meet ye, ma'am," he grinned, bowing profoundly. "And, lady"—he made another impressive bow to Mary—"the same to you." He turned to Dr. Shonto and Andy. "Gentle-*men*," he said, and bent nearly double again. "I am Shirttail Henry. They call me Shirttail because I live at Shirttail Bend, which is a hairpin curve in th' trail that leads from these here buttes here to the meadows up on top o' the mountains. My right name's Henry Richkirk, an' I ain't a nuisance in these parts, if I do say it myself. But I could name some that are, though I wouldn't. You," he continued, swinging back toward Charmian as if the wind had caught his fluttery garments and whisked him about, "are a gorgeous pretty girl, an' seein' ye stood up for Lot's Wife, I guess ye're perfect. If ye wanta make Shirttail Henry your friend, stand up f'r Lot's Wife. Ye done it, an' I'll tell ye somethin' about opals before ye go any furder. Shirttail Henry knows th' stones that've caught the colours o' the rainbow. An' he knows how they get them colours. Ye stood up f'r Lot's Wife, an' Shirttail Henry's gonta stand up f'r you. Nuisance, eh! Well—"

But here Smith Morley and Omar Leach leaped upon the man, and together they bore him, fighting, to the ground.

"He's crazy, Mrs. Reemy," puffed Leach, struggling to keep the big man on his back. "Crazy as a roadrunner. Dangerous, too! He's lived in this country all alone too long—and he's—"

At this point Dr. Inman Shonto and Andy Jerome took a hand in the rough proceedings.

CHAPTER VIII
MISSING

DESPITE the fact that there were two against him, the curious man from the mountains needed little aid. He was a powerful Cyclops, and his columnar arms flailed out to right and left as he fought on his back like a 'coon. He might have pounded off his enemies and gained his feet alone in time. But Andy had grabbed the coat collar of Omar Leach, and Dr. Shonto, himself a snarl of sinewy muscles, was in like manner dragging Smith Morley from the prostrate mountaineer. Charmian Reemy, biting her lips, looked on without a word. Mary observed proceedings with an acidulous smile, which might have signified any one of several primitive emotions.

While the doctor and Andy held the prospectors off, Shirttail Henry bounded to his feet and broadcasted a wide grin about the circle.

"You boys," he said to Leach and Morley, "come purty near goin' too fur that time. Some o' these days when ye get rambunctious with me, I'll take a stick and knock yer gysh-danged heads off. Heh-heh-heh!"

Despite the rather serious aspect of the situation, Charmian burst into a fit of laughter. Nothing could have been milder than the tone that Shirttail Henry used in reproaching his assailants. And his grin, together with the cackling laugh that followed his words of censure, took all of the menace out of his speech. Time and again in later days she was to hear Shirttail Henry utter dire threats of vengeance on some one, but invariably the sting was taken from his venomous tirade by the cracked "heh-heh-heh" that followed it.

Morley and Leach glowered at him, but made no further move to molest him. They knew that they were "in bad" with the prospective buyers of their mining properties, so they held their peace and did not struggle to free themselves.

It was Charmian who broke the silence that followed Shirttail Henry Richkirk's prophecy.

"This is a fine set of proceedings," she said witheringly. "Mr. Richkirk, if you care to, we'd like to have you camp with us to-night. We—I mean the greenhorns of the party—are ready and willing to do anything to make amends for the inhospitable treatment Mr. Leach and Mr. Morley have shown you. And if you feel inclined to tell me what you hinted at—about opals, you know—I'll certainly be glad to hear it."

But to her surprise Shirttail Henry had half turned from her and was gazing through a break in the buttes at the distant mountains. The moon was showering its pale radiance on the desert. Shirttail Henry extended one of his long arms and pointed to a tiny cloud above the distant range, which the moonlight now revealed.

"See that cloud?" he asked. "Well, that means Shirttail Henry and Lot's Wife have gotta go. I can't stay with ye to-night, ma'am—thank ye kindly. I gotta be gettin' to Shirttail Bend right quick, for maybe that cloud means rain. C'm'on, Mrs. Lot." He hurried to the burro and grabbed up the lead-rope. "Good night, people. I'll see ye maybe to-morrow, ma'am, an' tell ye about the opals. Good night, all—and thank ye kindly!"

With the newcomers staring after him in wonderment, he hustled his dejected pack animal out of camp, and they faded away into the desert night.

"Well, of all things!" gasped Mary Temple.

"You can see for yourselves," said Leach, with a note of doggedness in his tones, "that he's a regular nut. He's a hermit and lives all alone up there, not seeing anybody in months. He traps and fishes, and makes out in a disreputable cabin, with only his burro for company. He's the biggest nuisance imaginable, and, besides, he's dangerously insane."

"I don't believe that, Mr. Leach," Charmian declared, and set her red lips tightly after the words.

Leach shrugged. "Can't help that, Mrs. Reemy," he told her in a hurt tone. "But it's the truth. I don't want him in camp with me when I'm asleep. He might sneak up and cut my throat. The one thing on earth that I fear is a crazy man."

Andy and Dr. Shonto had released their captives, and now they silently sat down on the ground and awaited the outcome of the dialogue between Charmian and the opal miners. This was her adventure, and they did not wish to interfere so long as their opinions were not asked for.

"What did he mean about the cloud?" she asked.

"Oh, that," said Morley, and laughed shortly. "He is employed by the weather bureau to record the rainfall and snowfall in the section of the mountains where he lives. He gets seven or seven and a half a month—I forget just how much—for being on hand to read his rain gauge and sending in his reports. It's the most ridiculous thing you ever heard of, Mrs. Reemy. Henry will be away 'tending to his traps, and up comes a little cloud about the size of his ear. Then he drops everything and races home to his rain gauge, over which he'll squat until the cloud floats out of his section of the mountains. And when it does rain or snow he chases with his report all the way to Diamond H Ranch and sends it in to the weather bureau. And maybe while he's making the trip another cloud will show up. Then he's between the devil and the deep blue sea, for his report ought to go in at once, while at the same time more rain is threatening on his station. All that for not over seven and a half a month. Can you beat it! What do you think of him now? Is he crazy? And the kick he gets out of that job would make a horse laugh. He's always calling himself a goverment official; and when his check doesn't arrive promptly he writes a complaint to the President. Oh, Henry's a scream, all right!"

"He may be all of that," Charmian spoke thoughtfully, "but that's no excuse for mistreating him."

"Why, Mrs. Reemy—"

"I don't believe that I care to hear any defence of what you two men did tonight," she interrupted crisply. "Please let's drop the subject. I'm tired; I'm going to bed. Good night, everybody."

She walked away toward her tent, but paused suddenly, turned, and hurled back a parting shot.

"And I shall have a talk with Shirttail Henry before going any further into the buying of your opal claims."

Then she walked on out of the radius of the firelight glow.

It was dawn when Dr. Inman Shonto awoke. He crawled halfway out of his blankets and parted the tent flaps. Through the inchoate light he saw the gleam of the campfire and a figure moving about it. He heard the low rattle of pots and pans. The figure, he knew soon, was that of the industrious Mary Temple, and she was all alone.

The doctor himself had intended to rise first, rebuild the fire, and set water on to boil; but Mary had forestalled him. Provoked at himself for allowing a woman to rise first and begin the hard work of camp life, he struggled into his clothes without awaking Andy and hurried out to her.

"Good morning," he greeted her. "It's pretty shivery out here. You beat me to it, and I apologize for oversleeping and allowing you to start breakfast alone."

"You're a very considerate gentleman, Doctor," replied Mary Temple. "But this is nothing new for me, and I like to work. I like to smell the dawn come, too. They've gone."

"What's that? Who's gone, Miss Temple?"

"Leach and Morley and his wife," Mary replied, raking coals one side from the fire on which to place the coffeepot to simmer.

"Gone? Gone where?"

"Land knows! But I guessed it last night. They knew they'd not have any chance after Charmian talked with that Shirttail body. They're crooked, Doctor. A dog's hind leg would look like a steel ruler 'longside of Leach and Morley. I knew it—I just knew it all along!"

"Do you mean, Miss Temple, that Morley and his wife and Leach have ridden off and left us here on the desert?—that their opal claims are a fake, and that they were afraid Shirttail Henry would expose them to Mrs. Reemy?"

"Of course," answered Mary simply. "I knew it all along, but nobody would have paid any attention to me, so I couldn't say boo to a goose. Now isn't this a beautiful splatchet?"

"I don't believe I understand you," puzzled the physician. "A 'splatchet'?"

Mary never seemed to find the dictionaries adequate to the needs of her vocabulary. She invented words indiscriminately when the sound of them seemed to suggest the thought she wanted to express.

"A splatchet," she said carefully, "is a double mess on the floor. If you were baking pancakes, for instance, and turned to the sink a second to rinse out a couple of teacups, then saw that the pancakes were about to burn, and then you jumped for them and upset both the dishwater and the pancake batter, you'd make a splatchet on the floor."

"What animals have they taken?" asked Shonto, with a smile at her droll word coinage. "Have you investigated?"

"Of course," said Mary. "They've taken the three horses they rode here on, a little grub, and three canteens of water. That's all. No great loss to us. We've plenty left to travel back on. They tied what grub they took behind their saddles, for all the burros are here."

"You didn't find a note or anything like that?"

"Nothing."

"Well, this is a pretty mess, Miss Temple! Mrs. Reemy will be sick with disappointment."

"Maybe so. It'll do her good. If she'd taken my advice she'd be tucked in her pretty ivory bed at El Trono de Tolerancia this minute, and I'd be turning flapjacks at the fireplace. But, no—I don't know anything! Nobody listens to me!"

"To be quite frank with you," said the doctor, "I'm a little glad too that things have turned out like this. I hated to see Mrs. Reemy sink fifty thousand dollars in opal mines, so I offered to go in with her. So did Andy. But all three of us have about as much need for an opal mine as we have for two noses. Just the same, I was willing to put my shoulder under a third of the proposition to please Mrs. Reemy and help her out with her great adventure. But now, as I said, I'm rather satisfied that it has turned out as it has."

"You like to see the fire flash in her brown eyes when she talks about her big adventure, don't you, Doctor?" Mary Temple shot at him.

Dr. Shonto laughed, though by no means mirthfully. "What do you mean by that?" he asked.

Mary's faded eyes looked at him steadily, and the thin nostrils of her long nose twitched squirrel-like. "Oh, you know what I mean," she lashed out. "I can read the signs. Well, I never was a body to hold my tongue. I say what I think. And now I'm thinking that I'd rather see you get her than your friend Mr. Jerome. He may be all right, so far as men go, but he's too much like her to suit me. Too young and rattle-headed. You could tone her down a bit. But Jerome'll get her—that's plain. She's in love with him this minute. But it won't last, Doctor. There'll be a divorce if they marry. Then you can step in. But for my part I'd rather see her single."

"I think," said Shonto soberly, "that in your youth you must have sung an old ditty that comes to my mind—

"What are the little girls made out of?

What are the little girls made out of?

Sugar and spice and everything nice—

That's what the little girls are made out of.

"What are the little boys made out of?

What are the little boys made out of?

Rats and snails and puppy-dogs' tails—

That's what the little boys are made out of."

"You have a pretty good bass voice," was all that Mary said, as she began slicing bacon on the bottom of a bucket.

CHAPTER IX
A CASE FOR REJUVENATION

CHARMIAN REEMY received the news of the flight of Leach and the Morleys with equanimity.

"I have been afraid for some time," she asserted at breakfast, "that there was something wrong. Oh, well, it doesn't greatly matter. I never should have considered buying the opal claims, anyway, if it hadn't been necessary to do it in order to get the location of the Valley of Arcana. And Shirttail Henry ought to be able to at least show us how to get a peep at it."

"Charmian Reemy, you're going home," announced Mary stiffly.

"Wrong again, Mary Temple. We're going to find the Valley of Arcana and explore it."

"Then I'll not move another foot, Charmian. That's flat."

"So is the desert," said Charmian demurely, "and to spend the remainder of your life on it, Mary Temple, would be frightfully monotonous."

"You know what I mean well enough," snapped Mary. "I'll find a way to get home without you."

"Mary Temple, your miner's bread is simply exquisite this morning," Charmian told her placidly. "You haven't forgotten our delightful days in Alaska, I see. Mary Temple, hereafter I intend to refer to you as my companion at arms. You're so companionable that I couldn't think of existing without you, and you're always up in arms. Companion at arms is right. I'm glad I thought of that one. Naming things is my hobby, you know, Doctor."

"Charmian," quoth Mary in a sepulchral voice, "have you forgotten what Madame Destrehan saw in your Valley of Foolishness?"

"Let's see. It was a madman bending over me, wasn't it?—and stretching out his talonlike fingers toward my throat?"

"It was—and you know it. Well, haven't you had warning enough?"

"You are well aware, Mary Temple, that I put no faith whatever in the second sight of Madame Destrehan or any other swindler," Charmian reminded her.

"But in this case, isn't her prophecy working out? Haven't we had the madman right here in our camp? What better evidence of her powers can you ask for, Charmian?"

"In camp," said the perverse young widow, "I always take two cups of coffee for breakfast, Doctor. One with the trimmings, and one black. May I trouble you to pour me another cup? And do you really think Shirttail Henry is a nut, Mary Temple?"

"Putting aside what Leach and Morley told us about him," Mary replied, "didn't we see him strike off for the mountains when he saw a tiny cloud no bigger than a pancake? And think of him writing to the President when his puny little check fails to come on the dot! I wouldn't call him a nut. I wouldn't call anybody a nut, because that's vulgar. But he's a subject for a padded cell, and he'll choke you to death in your old Valley of Tomfoolery if you persist in going up there and giving him the chance."

"That would be a rather unique experience, don't you think, Andy?" asked the girl. "I've never even had a madman's fingers at my throat, let alone being choked to death by one. I think, if I barely succeeded in escaping alive, that my life would be fuller ever afterward. And if Henry wants to give me the delicious experience I mean to let him have his chance. But he mustn't overdo it. You'll keep close and see that Henry doesn't go too far, won't you, Doctor Shonto? When my tongue lolls out and I'm beginning to get blue in the face, just yell, 'Look at that cloud drifting over your rain gauge, Henry!'"

"Funny, ain't you?" sniffed Mary.

"Trying to be," said Charmian humbly.

The four ate in silence after this, Charmian's roguish brown eyes hidden by the long lashes. Now and then she looked up and smiled mischievously at Andy or the doctor, for all the world like a contrary little girl who knows she is exasperating and glories in it.

"When do we start?" asked Mary suddenly.

"For where?"

"For the mountains and Henry Richkirk's place."

"Why, we don't just know how to find him," said Charmian, winking at the two men. "But he's calling on us to-day, you'll remember. I guess we'll just have to stay here and wait for him. Well, we're all through eating, and I suppose, as hostess, I ought to rise first. But I'm so stiff from yesterday's ride. Won't you get up and help me on my feet, Andy?"

"'Mr. Jerome' would sound better, wouldn't it, Charmian?" There was a decided corrective note in Mary's tone.

"Oh, we can't bother with mistering and missising and missing one another," protested the girl. "I call Doctor Shonto 'Doctor,' and I've simply got to have a brief name for Mr. Jerome. Andy's mighty handy. And, if you don't mind,

I'd like to have you two gentlemen, or overgrown boys, or whatever you call yourselves, address me as Charmian. It takes all the kick out of camp life to go about mistering and missising one another. Which would sound more practical, Mary Temple?—'Doctor Inman Shonto, I think that rattlesnake is about to bite you' or *'Jiggers, Doc! Rattlesnake!'* I think our eminent physician would jiggers more promptly if he heard the latter, don't you? Why, I seem to be in pretty good spirits this morning, don't I?"

"You're talking a lot," said Mary, and rose to gather up the "dead and wounded" and place them in the dishwater.

The doctor had fed and watered the stock while Mary was completing her breakfast-getting. This ascertained, Charmian proposed a ride in search of the opal mines of their vanished dreams. They were only two miles farther in the buttes, the prospectors had revealed, and the girl wanted to visit them while they awaited the coming of the devoted weather man. Also, she wished to limber up again in preparation for the ride to the mountains. Mary Temple refused to be lured from the domestic duties of the camp, so the girl and the two men rode off without her.

As they started Mary shrilled after them:

"Andy Jerome—if I *must* call you Andy—did you forget to take your medicine this morning?"

Andy grinned sheepishly, stopped his horse, and dismounted.

"Humph!" sniffed Mary. "I thought as much."

Andy went to his tent and took a tablet from a pasteboard box. As he carried it to the spring for water to wash it down, he asked:

"How did you know I am taking medicine, Mary?—if I *must* call you Mary."

"Humph! Haven't I seen you swallow one of those little tablets regularly every morning since I first met you? And I know medicine must be taken regularly in order to get the full benefit of it. I don't know what you're taking those tablets for, and I don't care, but I do know that, so long as I am one of the idiots in this Bonehead Country, you'll not miss a morning while the medicine lasts."

"Thanks for your thoughtfulness, Mary," Andy laughed. "I don't wonder that Charmian finds you indispensable. But did you call the Shinbone Country the Bonehead Country by accident, or—"

"Or," Mary interjected decisively.

There was but one direction for the trio to travel, they found, because they were in a pass between the two lines of buttes. It was not long before they saw evidences of bygone mining activities—several dumps of rather large proportions, and above them tunnels in the side of a hill. They left their horses on the level land and clambered up among the rocks, to find that, in some past day, a great deal of work had been done.

They investigated for an hour or more, and then a voice hailed them from a distance, and they saw the gigantic figure of Shirttail Henry approaching along the floor of the pass. He came straight toward them, negotiated the hillside with ease, and made his profound bows all around when he reached them.

"No rain a-tall," he announced morosely. "That cloud was gone before I got there. I'm glad ye left Leach an' Morley behind. I wanted to talk to ye alone about these here claims here."

A few words sufficed to apprise him of the unexpected decampment of the designing opal miners, and the recital brought forth Shirttail Henry's cackling "Heh-heh-heh."

"I ain't a-tall s'prised, ma'am," he told Charmian. "They're ornery, them two boys. This ain't th' first time they tried to sell these ole abandoned opal mines to some one."

"Abandoned mines?" puzzled Charmian.

"Course," said Henry. "That's what they are. Twenty year ago they was a lot o' fine stones took outa here. There's lots o' opal here yet, but it ain't got any fire. Ye see, ma'am, it takes time for an opal to gather its fire. The fellas that staked out these claims got rich. I know they sold one stone they found for ten thousand dollars—one of the biggest prices ever paid for an opal. But the good stones run out, so they abandoned the claims. Then Leach an' Morley filed on 'em just to have somethin' to sell to some sucker. In time the opals here will gather their fire, but you folks wouldn't be here to mine 'em."

"How long does it take an opal to get its fire?" asked Charmian.

"Oh, matter of a hundred thousan' years," said Henry.

"Good night!" exclaimed the widow. "If we'd bought the claims, Doctor, you'd have had a good chance to prove the efficacy of rejuvenation by the gland treatment. Well, that for the opals!"—and she snapped her fingers. "They're unlucky, anyway. Mary Temple says so. Now, Mr. Henry, what do you know about an undiscovered or an unexplored valley somewhere up in the mountains?"

"I know she's there, ma'am—that's about as much," answered the mountaineer.

"Have you ever seen it?"

"Onct—from the top of a high peak. But nobody's ever been there. They tried it—lots of 'em—an' failed to make it. It can't be done. Who told ye about that valley—Leach an' Morley?"

"Yes," said Charmian. "But I don't agree with you when you say it can't be done. We'll pay you well to show us the valley from the peak that you mention, and for any hints or suggestions about reaching the valley that you can give us. Also, we want to find a certain mountain meadow that Morley told us of, where we can pasture our horses and such burros as we won't need in the undertaking. What do you say?"

"I'll help ye out," Shirttail Henry promised. "An' I'll tell ye all I know. That's more'n most of 'em in the Shinbone Country know, at that. But ye'll never make it, ma'am. When I take ye to th' top o' the peak, where ye c'n see all over this country, ye'll know I'm right."

"Well, we'll do our best, anyway," Charmian told him. "And we're ready to begin when you are."

"Poor time o' year to tackle a job like that. Better wait till May or June next year."

"We'll go as far as we can at any rate," Charmian decided. "Then if we fail we will know better how to go about it to succeed next summer."

"All right," said Henry. "I'm ready now."

"Then if you'll wait here for us we'll ride back and break camp at once. We haven't an extra horse for you, so—"

"I never fork a hoss, ma'am," Henry interrupted. "I c'n go where a hoss can't with these here ole legs here. You ride; I'll hoof it. Don't worry about Shirttail Henry gettin' there time yer hosses do, ma'am."

CHAPTER X
SHIRTTAIL BEND

SHIRTTAIL HENRY walked ahead up the mountain trail, Ichabod Crane come to life. His loose-jointed figure shuttled about as if the huge trunk were threatening to topple from the legs that shook it with their gigantic strides. His loose clothes fluttered in the wind, adding to the shimmylike effect. But Henry covered ground.

The four who had undertaken the exotic adventure followed on their horses, urging the complaining burros ahead of them. When practicable Charmian rode with Andy, Shonto with that attitudinized wet blanket known as Mary Temple.

Hours ago the party had left the level reaches of the desert. They now were ascending sharply into a rarer atmosphere, and the yuccas, cacti, sage and greasewood had surrendered to junipers, piñon pines, and an occasional taller conifer. The trail twisted about the heads of deep cañons in S curves, U curves, and abrupter V's. Now and then a break in the ever-thickening forest revealed the yellow desert below them like a gigantic slice of buttered bread. Birds and squirrels inhabited the trees. Once a big buck bounded across the trail ahead of them, tiny front hoofs touching his breast as he shot himself forward and upward like an airplane leaving the earth. The trees and the wild life made a pleasing relief from the barren wastes below.

For the remainder of the day they climbed, camping at noon on the trail. As the day drew toward its close they found themselves surrounded by a vast forest, primeval as Evangeline's, with no view of the desert offered. As dusk descended upon the mountains the trail began to grow painfully steeper, and then it swung about the brow of a rise in a long curve. Henry paused and looked back at his followers.

"This here long curve here is Shirttail Bend," he announced. "My cabin's just around th' corner."

The land rose sharply at the middle of the hairpin curve, and horses and burros panted as they struggled upward. They then reached a level shelf in the mountainside, a small plateau of perhaps five acres. In the centre of it, with the trail leading directly by, stood the tumble-down cabin of the erratic weather man.

The cabin was built half of logs, half of boards from the lumber mill. A huge stone chimney promised the warmth of an open fireplace within. Climbing vines fingered the walls of the structure. A spring above it was the source of a tiny stream that trickled across the dooryard and fed a mat of watercress. Henry had gooseberry bushes and currant bushes, and there was a pear and apple orchard of a dozen trees. The water from the spring eventually found its way into a man-made ditch, from which it seeped onto a small patch of frost-nipped alfalfa.

Henry's dooryard was cluttered with every imaginable thing that had seen its day, from a grindstone whose three remaining legs sagged rheumatically beneath it to a hay rake with one wheel and a depleted set of teeth. There were pieces of rusty iron of all descriptions, old sets of hames, wagon wheels, joints of gaspipe of all sizes and lengths, lopped-over wagon seats, one of which had been hung as a swing, innumerable chains, sleds, broken pack-saddles, chicken coops upside-down, spewing mattresses, axles, an ancient dresser minus its mirror and resting placidly on its back, the iron-and-wood pedestal of an office swivel chair—and from every tree hung chains, frayed ropes, wagon-seat springs, iron hounds, countless horseshoes, more hames and other fragments of harness, and steel traps of every size. All these treasures, Henry confided to his guests, he had brought in, piece at a time, on the back of Lot's Wife or his own sturdy shoulders, imagining that "sometime they might come in handy." Often he had been obliged to dismember the larger pieces of junk—the hay rake, for example—and pack them in by sections. "Un Rincon Confusión," Charmian promptly christened the place, which in Spanish is equivalent to "A Corner of Chaos." Mary called it a whompus—which, she interpreted, was either a dish that she made of left-over boiled potatoes, bread crumbs, and sage, or a dog's breakfast.

But the home was picturesque and quaint, and the smells of the virgin forest all about were sweet and bracing. The light mountain air hinted at frost. Innumerable birds twittered their good-night melodies in the treetops. Frogs croaked in satisfaction in the ditch that watered the alfalfa. A few hens troubled with insomnia loitered about the yard, crooning to themselves as they pecked hopefully at pebbles that looked like grain. The brook sang softly its unchangeable song of the days when the mountains heaved as the earth grew cold, the travail that gave it birth.

"Just make yerselves to home, folks," invited the mountaineer. "Ye c'n turn yer stock on th' 'falfy if ye ain't afraid o' founderin' 'em. Lot's Wife she don't care for 'falfy. She likes to browse offen th' sage an' bresh. I'll look at my rain gauge, an' then I'll chop some wood and we'll get a fire goin'."

He fluttered to the alfalfa patch and gave studious attention to something on the ground. Then he returned to the tired party, and sighing, "Not a drop!" he began helping to off-saddle the steaming animals.

The quartette left Henry to his own domestic serenity in the little cabin, themselves camping at a decent distance from the house on a spot where Henry had neglected to distribute his heterogeneous treasure trove. They built a cheery campfire, over which Mary Temple cooked supper. Then when

Shirttail Henry had rejoined them they settled down for a discussion of the morrow's undertaking.

"She's a rarin' trip," Henry said discouragingly. "First ye gotta finish climbin' this here mountain here, and then ye'll come on a level valley where they's a lake. They's salt grass and bluejoint around the lake, but the frost's ketched it by now, an' it'll be dryin'. Yer stock'll eat it, though, and fatten on it. An' that's th' place to pasture 'em till ye get back ag'in.

"So now we've disposed o' th' critters. An' then we hike across th' valley an' cut up a cañon on th' other side. In th' cañon they's a crick that empties into th' lake. Well, then we folly that crick for ten miles, maybe—an' it's a job. All boulders bigger ner my cabin, an' down trees an' th' like. Well, then we're pretty high up, an' now we cut across through th' timber towards Dewlap Mountain. That's where we're headin' for.

"Now and then we'll be seein' th' mountain, but not often. We gotta go by compass—at least you folks would. I go by guess and by gosh. Well, then, that's a matter o' twenty mile to th' foot o' th' peak, and up it's a heap more.

"Now not a few folks have made this side o' Dewlap Mountain, but mighty few ever got on th' other side. I done it, and so has Reed. That's th' forest ranger that first saw th' undiscovered valley. Gettin' 'round on th' other side o' the mountain is where th' rub comes in—that is, th' rubbin'est rub. The top o' th' peak's above th' line of perpetual snow, an' up there, besides, it's all rocks an' steep places till ye can't rest. It's skeery gettin' 'round to th' other side; an' many a time ye wisht ye hadn't come, when ye look down on what's below ye—or what ain't below ye. But I made her an' Reed he made her, an' ye gotta do it to see the undiscovered valley. But gettin' to the toes o' Dewlap Mountain ain't no fun neither."

Shirttail Henry came to a thoughtful pause. The firelight played on his kindly, rugged features as he sat tailor-fashion and gazed with his dreamy blue eyes into the blaze. His was almost a poetic face, Charmian thought, as she studied what was revealed of it above the flaring torch of whiskers.

"Seems to me," the mountaineer went on softly, "that, when all's said an' done, this time o' year'd be about th' best to tackle th' trip. Ye see, th' snow's been meltin' all summer, more or less, an' so fur this season they ain't any fell yet. So right now th' snow's at her shallowest depth up on that there mountain there. An' ye might get in an' out before snow begins to fly, if luck was with ye.

"And I thought of another thing: They was a big fire up in thataway this summer, an' maybe it took out a part o' th' big bresh stretches that lies between th' head o' the cañon an' th' toes o' Dewlap. If it done that th' trip'll be lots easier. But we'll know more time we tried her."

"Is it necessary to go over Dewlap Mountain to reach the Valley of Arcana?" asked Charmian.

"Well, no, 'tain't," replied the weather man. "Contrary to that, ma'am, she'd be a fool way to go about it. Ye go up there to see th' valley; but to get to her ye'd oughta go round th' mountain. That's th' way Reed went. He tried both sides. But he never made th' riffle. It can't be done."

"Why?"

"Chaparral that ye can't get through an' walls o' rock that can't be climbed."

"And how about Lost River?"

"That's another proposition, ma'am. Lost River's forty mile to th' north o' Dewlap Mountain, an' about th' same distance from yer Valley of Arcana. Over toward th' Alondra Country, where they's an Indian reservation that's got gold on it. Leach an' Morley they got run out for pannin' gold on that reservation, an' gov'ment agents was after 'em for a spell. That's how come it they know about Lost River, ma'am. But if Lost River runs through yer valley, that ain't no help to ye."

"I thought that perhaps we might build a canoe and drift down the river underground to the Valley of Arcana," Charmian stated simply.

"Holy sufferin' cats!" bellowed Shirttail Henry.

Even Andy and Dr. Shonto laughed at the girl's naïve assurance.

"You've been reading fantastic fiction, Charmian," said Andy. "That's a pipe dream."

"Perhaps," half conceded the young widow, unperturbed. She turned her brown eyes on Henry again. "But why climb to the peak of Dewlap Mountain merely to gain a view of the valley?" she asked. "Why not circle the mountain when we reach it and try for the valley itself?"

"Too late in th' season," Henry maintained. "Th' snow she'd ketch us, ma'am."

"I'm not afraid of snow. I've roughed it in Alaska. Any snow you'd have here would be a joke, compared with what I've experienced."

"Pretty cold joke sometimes," Henry remarked. "But I been thinkin' ag'in, ma'am: Reed he always tried to make th' riffle in summer, an' then th' snow over thataway's deepest. An' in winter blizzards are blowin', an' ye can't do nothin'. Same as in th' case o' gettin' to th' top o' Dewlap, right now would be th' easiest time to tackle th' valley trip, after th' snow's melted all summer long. I guess Reed thought o' that, but was afraid to tackle her with winter comin' on. If a body got ketched in that country after th' blizzards started—Say, none o' that in mine! He'd never come out, that's all."

"Nonsense!" scoffed the girl. "The chances are that Reed didn't have enough money to properly equip himself for a trip of that nature."

"No, Reed he ain't got anything but his pay from th' gov'ment—same as me. An' th' boys that tackled th' trip with him two three times, they never had nothin'. If a body could get enough supplies in th' country to stand a siege, come blizzard time, he might get through to th' valley between storms. He'd want skis or snowshoes, though—and a heap o' grub an' things. Once he made th' valley everything'd be jake. It's like summer down in there, I'm thinkin'."

"I can ski," Charmian announced. "So can Mary Temple. How about the rest of you?"

Dr. Shonto and Andy shook their heads. Henry professed familiarity with snowshoes, but never in his life had he been on skis.

"I reckon, after all," Henry decided, "that skis wouldn't do. Ye might enter th' Valley of Arcana too pronto fer yer health. Snowshoes would be safest. You two men could learn to use them in no time, after ye'd practised a bit."

"I'm for striking out direct for the valley to-morrow morning," Charmian said suddenly. "What's the use hemming and hawing about it? Nothing was ever accomplished by indecision. It's a chance, and we take it—that's all. If the storms were to hold off for any considerable time, Henry, how long ought it to take us for the trip in and out?"

"I can't tell ye, ma'am—never havin' finished her. But I'd say a month."

"*A month!* So long as that?"

"Outside time, ma'am," Henry explained.

"And is there any possibility of winter holding back that long?"

"Yes'm, they is. Ye never can tell what she's gonta do. I'm a United States weather man, an' I'm speakin' from experience. One year winter she'll set in as early as this. Next, they maybe won't be any snow to speak of before Christmas. We've had three early winters hand-runnin' now an' I'd say it's time for a late one."

"Will you go along, Henry, and show us the way?" the girl asked eagerly.

"I been thinkin'," Henry replied. "How'm I gonta tend to my weather reports?"

"Take your gauge along with you, can't you?"

"I dunno 'bout that," said Henry. "But if ye was to pay me well enough—"

"How much will your services be worth?"

Henry pursed his lips. "I get seven and a half a month for bein' weather man," he mused, "and, come next month, I'll have a line o' traps strung between Rustler Crick an' Palance Ridge. If I'm lucky, I oughta clean up a hundred dollars at th' traps th' month we'd be gone. An' then—"

"I'll give you two hundred and fifty dollars to take us to where we can continue on ourselves to the Valley of Arcana," Charmian interrupted.

"Well-l-l—" Shirttail Henry Richkirk puckered his lips doubtfully.

"Or until we give up in despair," Charmian supplemented.

Henry rose briskly from the fireside. "Be up an' fed by six o'clock," he said. "I'll be ready."

He started to flutter toward his cabin when the sharp voice of Mary Temple stayed his steps.

"Where are your snowshoes? Where is any grub sufficient to take these idiots on a trip like that?" she demanded.

"Well, now, ma'am," replied the weather man, "I think we c'n git more snowshoes at Mosquito Ranch, which is halfway up this here mountain here from my place to th' lake. I got two good pair myself. An' we c'n git a beef critter killed for us at the ranch an' freeze th' meat an' take a lot of it along with us. Besides, I got a lot o' jerky, which comes in mighty handy when everything else has give out."

"Have you any soap?" asked Mary crisply.

"Why, yes'm—I got a whole case of her that's never been opened."

"Take it along," said Mary.

"Why, Mary Temple!" cried Charmian. "What need have we for a hundred cakes of soap? Think of the weight it will add to the pack, which weight ought to be composed of something to eat."

"Henry himself will need half a case," said Mary. "Don't for a minute imagine, Charmian Reemy, that I mean to live like an Indian on this fool trip. Supplies are supplies, and no supplies are complete without an ample amount of soap. Henry, did you think about the snowshoes and the beef when you proposed setting off at six o'clock to-morrow morning?"

"Well, now, no'm," Henry confessed, shifting his great weight from one huge foot to the other. "Maybe I just didn't," he added weakly.

"And you didn't want to go until Charmian promised to pay you even if the expedition failed, did you?"

"I didn't say that, ma'am," poor Henry tried to defend himself.

"No, you didn't. But your legs did when you jumped up so suddenly. Henry, do you know that, probably because of your great service to the government as weather man, the United States Navy has a war ship named after you?"

Henry's blue eyes bugged. "No'm, I didn't," he gasped. "D'ye honestly mean to tell me they got a ship they call th' Richkirk?"

"No," said Mary Temple. "It's called the Marblehead. Good night."

CHAPTER XI
THE TRAIL TO MOSQUITO

ANDY JEROME was up early the following morning, even before Shirttail Henry was astir. He went to the creek, broke a thin sheet of ice, and washed his hands and face. Then, quite proud of his achievement, he stepped briskly back to camp to start a fire, only to find that newly laid kindling had been lighted while he was at his toilet.

Now came Mary Temple, her lean arms encircling a big load of Henry's firewood, proving that she herself was still supreme as the early riser of the party.

"Well, Mary, you're a wonder!" Andy praised her. "I thought that for once I'd beaten you to it. Good morning."

"Get another armload of wood," said Mary. "Good morning."

Andy returned from the wood pile and let his burden clatter on the ground.

"What's for breakfast?"

"Beans."

"Good! Beans are the stuff in camp, all right."

"They're the stuff in the Palace Hotel," said Mary. "Beans conquered the West. They won the war. They're—"

"Oh, don't tell me about the marvellous bean," Andy cut in. "I've always been a bean hound. And I'll bet you can cook 'em, too. You're a wonderful cook, Mary, do you know it?"

"I've hinted as much to myself a couple of times," Mary sniffed. "But I'm nothing compared with my brother Ed." Mary was diligently searching in a pack-bag as she talked.

"That so?"

"Yes, Ed was a master cook—a chef. He worked for one of the big bean-canning factories back East until they fired him."

"That was too bad," Andy sympathized. "What was the difficulty?—if I'm not too inquisitive."

"Ed killed a woman," Mary explained, still fumbling in the bag.

Andy said nothing; the topic of their conversation seemed to be growing a little delicate.

"Killed a woman he'd never seen," Mary added.

"Mary Temple, are you trying to kid me?" asked Andy warily.

"To this day we don't know her name," Mary went on, still searching. "But we know Ed killed her."

"Spring it—I'll bite. How'd he kill her?"

"He put two bites of pork in a can of pork and beans instead of one," said Mary. "And I know the woman that opened that can dropped dead. Anyway, they fired Ed for wasting the company's profits."

She stood erect with a can-opener in one hand and a large can labelled Pork and Beans in the other, and without a smile began the conflict between them. "Better wake the doctor," she advised. "The wonderful cook will have breakfast ready in no time this morning. She and you and the doctor can draw straws for the pork—I don't care for it. Here comes the good ship Marblehead."

Andy chuckled. He liked this droll, gaunt Mary Temple who was so devoted to the girl he loved. "And do you never expect to find more than one bite of pork in a can of pork and beans?" he asked.

"I'd as soon think of finding the Valley of Arcana," Mary replied.

With a brief "Good mornin', ma'am" Shirttail Henry passed Mary Temple at the campfire and went to his tumble-down stable. When Andy had awakened Dr. Shonto and had received a feeble response to his call from Charmian, he returned to Mary, to find Henry there with a slim sledge that he had found among his belongings.

"Thought she might come in handy," he grinned. "If we c'n pack her on one o' th' burros, she'll carry all our truck when we leave the critters and keep on afoot. Can't use her, though, lessen it snows. But I thought we'd better take her along."

"Good idea," said Andy lightly, and turned to Mary, who was pointing to a small die of fat pork, a tiny monument in the pan of sizzling beans.

"I found it," she announced grimly.

A great deal of time was consumed after breakfast in packing the twelve burros, for among the party only Shirttail Henry was an expert at the art. He was careful in his preparations, and when all was ready for the start nobody could think of anything necessary that he had omitted from the pack. He hazed the little animals into the trail and followed them on foot, the remainder of the party bringing up the rear on their saddle horses.

The morning was crisp, the air tingling with frost. The thud of the animals' hoofs came clear and distinct, for the ground was frozen and an uncanny hush dwelt in the heavy forest through which they passed. The saddle horses frisked about, shying at this and that familiar object, and their nostrils shot forth white steam, even as the nostrils of fearsome dragons shoot forth smoke and fire and brimstone. Squirrels scurried rattlingly over dead leaves from their interrupted breakfasts, to twitch their grey plumes and wrinkle their muzzles at the travellers from the security of lofty branches.

"Great morning to start our adventure," commented Andy Jerome, as they came upon a wide stretch of trail and he urged his horse to the side of Charmian's.

"Absolutely perfect," Charmian agreed. "My, but my feet are cold! Andy, I wonder if we *are* absolute idiots, after all. Sometimes I think that, if Doctor Shonto weren't with us to lend the expedition an air of dignity and—well, consequence—I'd lose my nerve. You and I are mere kids, and don't really know whether we have any business to undertake this thing or not. But Doctor Shonto is a man of brains and experience—a somebody—and it bolsters up my courage a lot to know that he is with us and seems to approve. Were you surprised at his coming along?"

"Yes," said Andy shortly.

"I wonder why he did come," mused the girl.

"That's a simple question to answer," Andy told her with boyish sulkiness. "He came because of you."

She looked at him quickly, then lowered her eyes. Charmian knew perfectly well that Andy Jerome was in love with her, and this knowledge did not distress her in the least. She did not know whether or not she was in love with Andy, but she knew that she liked to have his admiring eyes upon her and to note the little caress in his tones when he spoke to her in lowered accents. She knew now that Andy bitterly resented his friend's interest in her. But, of course, womanlike, she pretended innocence.

"Do you think the doctor is interested in me?" she asked.

"Humph!"

"Why?—do you suppose?"

"Heavens and earth, Charmian! Wouldn't any he-man be interested in a woman like you?"

Charmian took a bold step. She was no unsophisticated débutante, this young widow from Alaska. The relations between the sexes were no closed book to her. She was modernly ready and willing to discuss the tender passion. It was an integral part of life, and no false modesty caused her to shrink from facing any of the realities. Furthermore, she was a woman, young and pretty and desirable, and she liked to utilize her world-old heritage of making all men admire her.

"You don't for a moment imagine that Doctor Shonto is in love with me, do you?" she asked, round-eyed.

"Humph! Of course he is. And you know it as well as I do, Charmian."

She threw back her head and laughed, while Andy watched her frosty breath and suffered silently.

"How ridiculous!" she exclaimed. "To think that a man of the calibre of Doctor Inman Shonto could consider me in such a light as that. Andy, you're a scream!"

"Then why *is* he with us?"—still gloomily.

"That's just what I'm trying to find out. But your answer is silly—stupid, Andy. But I suppose the novelty of the thing appeals to him, as it does to you and me. After all, the doctor is not so old. I find him quite naïve and boyish at times. Only thirty-four. Why, a man shouldn't begin to think of being serious until he has passed fifty. Henry Ford says, even, that he ought not to begin to accumulate money until he's over forty. That from probably the richest man in the world! And the doctor doesn't look a day over twenty-five, does he?"

"I've never given his age much thought," said Andy with impolite abruptness.

"Don't you feel well this morning, Andy? You seem so sort of grouchy."

"I'm feeling fine," said Andy in the same stiff tones.

There was a smile of vast complacency on Charmian's lips as she looked away from him off through the towering pines. She wondered if she loved this boy, who carried his heart so openly on his coatsleeve. He certainly was attractive in his handsome young manhood. He would make an ardent lover. But what else, she wondered? He seemed to do little or no thinking for himself. He just took life lightly and let things slide, never worrying, never striving for anything, never revealing any depth of soul in any of his varied moods. His family was well off, and he did not have to work. Neither did she have to work, for that matter; but she did work. She worked her mind. She pondered over many things. She forced herself into deep reveries, reveries which were not consumed with egotism. She thought of life and the problems of humanity, and always she strove to think constructively. And thinking is the hardest work that one can do.

Andy loved her—or thought he did. Quite well was she aware of that. And it pleased her. She wanted fine young men to love her. She could not help it. She—*they*—are born that way. Would men have it otherwise?

But Dr. Shonto! The radiance with which the morning had endued her transparent skin was heightened by the glowing thought. If she had swayed Shonto, either by her physical or her mental or her plain womanly charms, or all these combined (herself, in short), she had made a conquest to be proud of. Of course to marry him was out of the question entirely. The gulf of years was between them. But it was warmly satisfactory for her to realize that a man of his importance had entered into her novel little game of make-believe discovery, and that he had not decided to come until she had assured him that she was serious in her desire to undertake the trip. And she was in nowise depressed over the thought that there was the remote possibility of her being in the wilds, on the great, romantic adventure of which she had dreamed so many times, with two seemly men who both were in love with her. Born romancer that she was, Charmian Reemy could not have pictured, in her most fantastic dreams, a situation more likely to add a wondrous and thrilling page to a life that she had long ago decided to make as novel as she could.

On up the trail the party forged, the labouring burros ahead, nibbling at this and that prospective edible along the way. The sun climbed high and sucked the frost from the stiff, chilled leaves. A clear sky overhung the mountains, and all was still. A stone clattering into a deep cañon made much ado, for the reverberations of its fall came hollowly to the listeners' ears. The bark of a squirrel as he revelled in the doubtful warmth of the autumn sun was heard for miles, for the mountains were steeped in that solemn hush that almost seems to sigh for another summer that has gone, a hush that bespeaks resignment to the dead days of winter yet to come.

And so to Mosquito they came, and camped there in the middle of a half glad, half melancholy afternoon that dreamed its short hours away in golden silence.

CHAPTER XII
THE LAND OF QUEER DELIGHTS

THEY left Mosquito the next morning, their pack replenished with a generous supply of beef. Also, as the mountain ranch had a quantity of stores on hand, they were allowed to purchase enough to bring their supplies up to the limit of the burros' carrying capacity. So now, over a hundred miles from the desert ranch where they had left the automobiles and at the beginning of their gruelling march to the Valley of Arcana, they were as well equipped for the ordeal as at the very start.

Four hours from Mosquito they topped the summit of the ridge, and looked down upon a smiling lake three miles in length by one in width. A carpet of dying grass surrounded the lake, near which but few trees grew, because of the strongly alkaline soil. They wormed their way down to the floor of the level mountain valley, and here they loosed the saddle horses and cached their equipment in a near-by cañon. Shirttail Henry guaranteed that the animals would not stray from the grazing ground. Once more he took the lead, and, driving the reluctant burros ahead of him, worked around the eastern end of the lake.

When they had completed a half-circle of the sheet of blue water and were on the south side opposite the grazing horses, Shirttail Henry made an abrupt turn to the left and hazed the string of burros up a little creek. For two miles or more the creek flowed through virtually level land, with mountain meadows on either side of it. Then gradually the land grew steeper, and the creek banks narrowed. The forest grew denser as they left the valley, and before half an hour had passed they were in a country as wild and rugged as that below Mosquito Ranch.

They camped for a late nooning before attempting the fierce climb that awaited them. When the burros had browsed an hour they were away again, up the ever narrowing cañon.

The little creek was a plunging torrent now, leaping over boulders, bellowing madly about snarls of ancient driftwood. Often there stood in the burros' path a huge boulder or outcropping that it seemed impossible for them to surmount, but Henry always found a way to get them over or around each obstacle. The burros climbed like goats when forced to it. Several times the men were obliged to take off their pack-bags so that they could squeeze through some gateway between gigantic stones.

The party was still in the cañon when the early mountain night closed down upon them. They fortunately had come upon a tiny level spot on which there was room to move about with comfort. Here they camped to await the coming of another day.

The night was cold and still, the sky cloudless. Nevertheless Shirttail Henry set up his rain gauge, muttering that he could not imagine how he was to send in his report if the gauge showed moisture in the morning. But no rain or snow fell to discomfit him, and the weary trailers passed the night in peace.

An hour after sunup the following day they came to the end of the cañon, to find that the source of the creek was a series of springs in a hillside. From the springs Henry set a course southwest through unbroken forest land, across which the going would have been easy but for the fact that the trail led continually up and down over a seemingly endless system of ridges. The party would struggle wearily up one steep hill, only to be obliged to clamber and slide down the other side of it into a deep V-shaped cañon—and then up the near side of another hill as steep as the one just mastered. Then down again, and up again—forever and ever, it seemed.

"Henry," said Mary, as they stood panting on the top of about the fifteenth rise that they had negotiated, "is this ever going to end?"

"Why, yes'm," Henry told her meekly. "These here little rises here get bigger and bigger until we're top o' th' mountains. Then we begin to crawl."

"Crawl!" puffed Mary. "I've done nothing else but crawl up and slide down since we left the creek back there. I don't feel like a human being any more. I'm a four-footed beast. I growl and show my teeth when a rock or a root gets in my way."

"But what I'm talkin' about," said Henry patiently, "is reg'lar crawlin'. Sure enough on yer hands an' knees, ma'am. An' f'r miles an' miles at that. Th' patch o' chaparral we'll have to go through ain't got its match in th' whole West, I'm thinkin'."

"Do you mean, Henry, that we're actually to *crawl* for miles and miles? Like a father playing bear with his baby on the floor?"

"Jest crawl, ma'am," replied Henry softly. "Unless we cut our way through with th' axes—an' that would take forever 'n' ever 'n' after."

"And you realize that, do you, Charmian?" Mary asked of the head of the party.

"Oh, yes—it's all been explained to me," Charmian assured her.

"All right," said Mary. "Then let's find a place to eat. I'm so hungry I could eat quirkus."

"Which is?"—Andy's question.

"Quirkus," Mary explained, "is the stuff you skim off the top of a kettle of fruit when you're cooking it for canning. Or it's the stuff that grows on the bottom of a watering trough in summer. Or sometimes it's any soft stuff that you don't know the name of, and that isn't fit to eat, but looks too valuable to throw away."

They spent two nights in the forest, forging onward throughout the short, cold, crystal days in the same southwesterly direction, up and down, up and down, but always gaining in altitude. They had left the Canadian Zone and were well into the Hudsonian, which constitutes the belt of forest just below timberline. Lodgepole pine, Alpine hemlock, silver pine, and white-bark pine had replaced the Jeffrey pine, red firs and aspens of the life zone immediately below them. They were over eight thousand feet above the sea, Henry told them, when at last, about ten o'clock of the third day after leaving the creek, the woods began to grow thinner, and they encountered frequent patches of short chaparral, bleak and rugged and rock strewn. They were entering the Arctic-Alpine Zone, comprising an elevation of from ten thousand five hundred feet to the tops of the highest peaks.

On and on, always climbing higher into an atmosphere more breath-taking, more crystalline. The chilled silences became awesome. Unfamiliar growths presented themselves, stunted, grotesque. An occasional patch of snow was crossed. A snow-white bird as large as a pigeon fluttered down to their camping ground, cocked his head on one side, and surveyed them with comical curiosity. A few grains of rolled barley, left by the wasteful burros, lay on the ground, for a small quantity had been brought along to tempt them back to camp when they wandered, browsing throughout the nights. The white bird pecked contemplatively at these, chattered his bill over one, and dropped it as unfit for avian consumption. As he hopped about, still intent on trying the unfamiliar particles that looked like food, his course took him directly over the foot of Charmian, who was standing very still and watching him. Utterly without fear of these human beings, he hopped upon the toe of her hiking shoe, and from that vantage point lifted his body and gazed about as a robin does for worms.

"The dear thing!" breathed the girl. "I guess he's never before seen a human being, and can't have any conception of what brutes we are. I wonder if I could pick it up!"

"Try it," urged the doctor softly.

Charmian stooped, her hands outspread. The movement caused the bird to hop from her shoe, but it did not make away. The girl stooped lower and lower, outspread fingers on either side of it. Her hands closed in to within six inches of the warm, white body. The bird looked up at her and hopped off sedately, without a sign of fear, but as much as to say, "Familiarity breeds contempt."

"I could have grabbed it, but I wouldn't!" maintained the widow. "But I *did* just want to touch it once!"

They decided that their visitor was an albino robin, probably a native of the regions above the line of perpetual snow, and that never before had it seen a human being.

"It makes me sort of shuddery," said Mary Temple. "That's no way for a bird to act, even if he is a country jake. It isn't right that he shouldn't be afraid of us. It's uncanny—and this is getting to be mighty uncanny country. Things get queerer and queerer every day, and I feel queerer and queerer every hour. I can just barely breathe in this light air. My head is on a spree and my feet are dead drunk."

"It only goes to show," argued Charmian, "how the wild creatures would consider us if only we were as decent as they are. There is no reason on earth why any wild thing should fear a human being. I have read arguments built up about the hypothesis that wild animals fear man instinctively, that they naturally recognize him as their master. More of man's monumental egotism! When an animal distrusts man, that distrust is bred in him by reason of his ancestors having been obliged to escape from human ruthlessness. Or the individual itself has suffered at the hands of man."

And not many days had passed before she proved, in part at least, that her contentions were correct; for the farther they forged into that untamed wilderness the more trusting the wild life became. Small, queer birds which none of them could name, most of them with long bills and heads that seemed almost as large as their bodies, followed them on the trail, perched above them in the chaparral and cocked their heads one side to stare down in puzzlement, and often flew to their very knees or alighted on their shoulders.

Upward and ever upward, over the sprawling toes and then over the generous knees of Dewlap Mountain. The only bird seen now was an occasional rosy finch; the mammals encountered consisted of the Alpine chipmunk, the grey bushy-tailed woodrat, and that quaint and ingenious native of the bleak altitudes, the Yosemite cony. This little animal, called variously rock rabbit, little chief hare, pika, or cony, is less than seven inches over all, and, much more so than the rabbit, has a tail which "mustn't be talked about." It has short rounded ears, dense hair, and, though closely resembling the rabbit, it runs an all fours, with a hobbling gait. It never sits up on its haunches, as does the rabbit, nor does it leave the Alpine Zone for a warmer clime when blizzards rage. Its home is in rock slides, where it cuts, dries, and stores up hay for use when the land is covered deep with snow. Often the travellers saw one perched on a lofty granite rock and heard its strange bleating cry of alarm.

The actinic quality of the light in this Boreal Zone made the few plants that the trailers came upon present rare, pure colours delectable to the eye. Most of these plants were cushion plants, spread out over the barren rocks where a little soil had gathered, and from the centre of the cushion the flower stalks arose. The doctor named the golden draba, the Alpine flox, and others; but the yellow columbine—not a cushion plant—was most remarkable of all. On the highest peaks flourished the Alpine buttercup, the Sierra primrose, and small Alpine willow trees, not above an inch in height. And at the very outskirts of snow banks they discovered the steer's head, a queer relic of pre-glacial times, whose flowers, modestly lopped over, resembled the heads of a sleepy bunch of cattle. Often this flower grew with snow all about it and seemed to thrive.

They were in a land of nothingness—cold and bleak and comfortless. On all sides wastes of loose stones and snow patches swept away from them. About them were the lofty peaks, so diamond clear in their dazzling whiteness that it pained the eye to look at them. They were crossing the knees of Dewlap mountain, making toward the south. They camped on windswept reaches, their mattresses the cold, hard rocks. Melted snow formed their water supply, and fuel that they had picked up in the warmer zone below them was nursed with miserly discretion.

After a day and a night in this forbidding land Shirttail Henry loosed the burros, for nothing grew for them to eat except the inch-high dwarf willows, and these were few. Burros will continue content for days and days without food or water, but Charmian demanded their release after twenty-four hours of deprivation. With indignant snorts, they kicked up their heels, and the bell burro set a bee-line course over the backward trail. When they reached the Hudsonian Zone, Henry said, they would browse their way gradually down through the Canadian, and into the Transition, where they would find an abundance of chaparral; and later they would reach the horses at the lake and remain close to them until snow drove the entire band to the lower contours, from whence they might wander even to the home ranch on the desert.

A rather serious catastrophe overtook the United States Weather Bureau on the day before the burros were released. Shirttail Henry had installed his rain gauge for the night, and had no more than turned his back on it when the bell burro was attracted by the brightness of its brass. She approached it with mincing steps, and, as is the custom of her kind, began trying to eat it. A burro seems incapable of deciding whether an object is for food by looking at it or smelling of it. He starts in to eat it, assuming that all things are good to eat until proved otherwise. The burro soon decided that in this instance she had made a grave mistake, and forthwith dropped the gauge. But not until the thin cylinder of brass had been dented and pinched in so that, as a recorder of the fall of rain, it was absolutely useless.

Mary Temple witnessed the desecration, but shouted too late. Henry wheeled in time, however, to capture the miscreant. He held her by the leather band that encircled her neck, and to which her tinkling bell was fastened, and looked her fiercely in the eye.

"Ass," he said, "ye ain't my canary, an' I know ye ain't got no sense. But if ye *was* mine, d'ye know what I'd do to ye? I'd hold ye by this here strap here, an' I'd get me a club, an' I'd take it an' I'd knock yer gysh-danged head off. Heh-heh-heh!"

Snow covered the greater part of the land where the explorers had loosed the asses. Henry rigged up his drag, and on it stowed the outfit. Henry and Andy took the lead ropes, and Dr. Shonto walked behind to push. By following a zigzag course the leaders were able to keep the sledge running upon snow for the greater part of the time, and when only bare rocks lay before them the party portaged the cargo and the sledge to snowy stretches beyond.

Their up-and-down course continued, and many a slope taxed the strength of all to get the laden sledge to the summit. But the general trend was downward, for they were crossing the knees of Dewlap, the only divide which gave access to the country wherein lay the mysterious valley of their quest. Gradually, after days of slow travel, the snow patches grew fewer and fewer, and the air grew noticeably warmer as they worked downward into the Hudsonian Zone once more. Then altogether the snow disappeared; scattering trees greeted them, Alpine hemlocks, silver pines—trees more friendly, it seemed to the awed wanderers, than any they ever had seen before. They saw a wolverine—infrequent animal—a white-tailed jackrabbit, and on one rare day a pure white squirrel, with pink-lidded eyes, quite curious and friendly.

They discarded the sledge, cached such tin-protected provisions as they could not carry on their backs, and forged on into a land of growing delights. They left the semi-bleak Hudsonian Zone above them and entered the friendly Canadian, where the Yosemite fox sparrow, the Sierra grouse, and the ruby-crowned kinglet greeted them; and among the mammals the jumping mouse, the yellow-haired porcupine, the Sierra chickaree, and the navigator shrew. The forest was heavy again, and there was firewood and the shelter of companionable conifers. Straight into the south Shirttail Henry led the way, down into a gigantic cup of the mountain range where grasses grew and sunlight flooded the land.

The forest became patchy, broken by occasional mountain meadows, rubble slides, cañons through which fires had spread their devastation and left sentinel trees and slopes covered with chaparral. Deep, impassible gorges forced them miles and miles to the east or the west, and sometimes turned them in the direction from whence they came. And in descending into one of these, after having followed its grim lip for many miles in search of a crossing, the redoubtable Mary fell, rolled down a steep incline, and terminated her mad descent in an ice-cold creek.

"Well," she remarked, as her anxious friends stumbled and slid down to her, "it's lucky I landed close to water, for right here I stay until the rest of you forsake your life of sin and come back to me on your way home. I've sprained my ankle terribly. Two of you hold me while Doctor Shonto pulls my leg."

CHAPTER XIII
AT TWO IN THE CAÑON

THOUGH the afternoon was not far spent, the party immediately went into camp in the gorge. If Mary's sprain was severe, the doctor told the others gravely, it would be impossible for her to touch the injured foot to the ground for many days. The men might carry her back, but it would be next to impossible, and altogether reckless, to carry her forward. What were they to do?

Mary was suffering silently beside the campfire, and the others had withdrawn to a distance to hold their conference. Then came her snappy voice:

"That's mighty impolite. I know what you're talking about. Come over here by the fire and I'll relieve your minds."

When they had congregated about her she said placidly:

"Now, there's just one thing for you to do. That is to go on, and leave me here in the cañon with enough grub to last me until you give up hope of ever finding the Valley of Tomfoolery. Which will be in a few days, at most, I'm thinking."

"Mary Temple," Charmian told her firmly, "we'll do nothing of the sort. We'll stay with you till you can walk or carry you over the back trail right now—and that ends that. We were only trying to decide which of the two would be the better plan."

"Charmian," said Mary, "will you kindly remember that it is *my* ankle that is sprained. I'm running that ankle myself, and whatever I say that has that ankle for a subject goes. This is not the first time that I have been in the wilderness, and a little thing like this doesn't trouble me in the least. This expedition, foolish though it is, means a lot to you. And I'm not going to allow you to come this far and have to give up because of me. You'll see this thing to the bitter end or I'll never move from this country, this cañon, this fireside, or this rock on which I'm sitting. You, and all of you—even old Marblehead—have browbeaten me, bullied me, overrun me since we lost those rascals, Leach and Morley, on the desert. But now at last, because of my sprained ankle, I am in command of the situation. And I mean to be obeyed. You'll leave me here, with provisions and an ample supply of firewood within arm's reach, while you continue on to the end of the Bonehead Country. You're not going to all this expense and deprivation and hardship for nothing. The sky's still clear. Henry's late winter seems assured. You may not have another chance in years to even come as far as you have. And you're going to shoot the piece while you're about it."

"Why, Mary Temple!" laughed Charmian. "What atrocious slang!"

"It's time for slang," Mary declared testily. "Shoot the piece!"

"But, Mary, it's perfectly—perfectly *hideous* to leave you here in this God-forsaken wilderness all alone—and you a woman with a sprained ankle. Neither the doctor nor Andy will consent to such a thing."

"They'll either go one way and leave me, or go the other way and leave me. This rock on which I'm sitting is my throne, and I won't move from it until I have my way. I'll die right here on this rock, I tell you, before I'll give in one inch!"

"But a mountain lion might attack you, Mary Temple!"

"Go on! You talk as if I were good to eat! Lions don't kill for the fun of it; they kill for meat. Only rats eat leather."

Dr. Shonto was regarding her thoughtfully. His examination of her ankle had puzzled him. It was not swelling, and when he felt the bones he had been unable to detect any evidence of sprain whatever. But her contorted features and white lips spoke plainly of pain. Now Mary surprised him by winking at him desperately, and, wondering, he held his peace.

"Now all of you but Doctor Shonto go up the cañon, around that bend, and stay there till we call you," ordered Mary. "Maybe you can talk some sense into one another's heads. I want the doctor to examine my ankle, and I'm too modest to have the bunch of you staring at me."

With a queer look at Shonto, Charmian led the way up the cañon for Henry and Andy, and they went out of sight around the bend.

"Well, Mary, what's all this about, anyway?" asked the doctor. "You haven't sprained your ankle, and you know it as well as I do."

"Of course not," replied Mary complacently. "But I've broken at least a couple of ribs."

"What!"

"I didn't want Charmian to know."

"Are you in pain?"

"Doctor," said Mary, "if you ever tell Charmian that I said what I'm going to say I'll never, never speak to you again. *It hurts like hell!* There—now you know, I guess."

"Well, for the love of Mike!" gasped Shonto. "Let me help you into your tent. Strip to the waist in there, while I rummage through the pack for my supplies."

"I don't need your help," snapped Mary. "You forget that my ankle isn't sprained. I can walk, but I can't *crawl*. And we're getting close to the crawling ground, Henry tells me."

"Oh, I understand," said Shonto.

Nevertheless he helped her to her feet and held her arm as she walked slowly and painfully to her and Charmian's tent. The doctor pawed through the pack, found his medicine case, and brought forth a tin spool of wide adhesive plaster. A little later, stripped to the waist and blushing furiously, Mary Temple came from the tent and stood before him.

Shonto's skilful fingers kneaded her torso as gently as possible, but Mary's lips were colourless and beads of perspiration stood out on her forehead.

"That hurt?"

"Humph! Of course!"

"And that?"

"I guess you know it does as well as I do."

"Well, Mary, I guess you've cracked one of them," remarked Shonto, after his careful examination.

He stepped behind her and flattened one end of a strip of adhesive plaster at the middle of her back, then brought it around to her right side.

"Now get all the breath out of you," he ordered. "Deflate your lungs as much as possible."

Mary took a deep breath, and then obediently blew lustily through her white lips until her lungs were free of air. As her chest went down, Shonto put his strength on the plaster and brought it around the front of her body, binding her tight. He put on one more strip, then told her he could do nothing else for her—that the plasters would hold the rib in place while it was knitting, and that, at her age, nature would not complete this process until the end of about three weeks.

"Don't let Charmian know anything about it," cautioned Mary, coming from the tent again. "I'll keep on pretending that I sprained my ankle. She'd worry if she knew I had a rib broken. And I could manage to walk back this way, couldn't I, Doctor?"

"Yes, if you walked slowly and carefully you might get by."

"That's what I thought. In fact, I've had a broken rib before, and while it pained me a lot—especially in bed at night—I was able to move around. So make Charmian think my ankle is sprained and that I can't walk a step. Then she'll think it's just as well for the rest of you to go on for a few days as to turn back—seeing that I can't walk either way. As I said, however, I can walk, after a fashion, but I can't crawl a single inch. You get the idea, don't you? I don't want to break up the expedition."

"But, Mary," he reminded her, "you have been against it from the start. It strikes me that now you have an excellent excuse to call it off."

"Oh, I'm against everything, Doctor," she chuckled grimly. "At first, anyway. I have to be to keep Charmian from going to extremes. Did you think for one moment, back there at El Trono de Tolerancia, that I'd allow her to go on this wild-goose chase without me? Not in a thousand years! And last night, before we went to sleep, she told me something, with her head resting on my lean old shoulder, that would keep me going to the end of time if she asked it."

"And what was that?" asked Shonto.

"Well, that queer country we just passed through seemed to work a sort of spell over her. Up until we struck the high altitudes this thing has been more or less of a lark with her. But up there, it seems, the queer things she saw made her mighty thoughtful. That was a weird, queer country, you'll admit yourself. It gave me the creeps; but it fired Charmian with the realization that this is, after all, a big undertaking, and that there's nothing foolish or childish about it.

"Charmian always wanted to do something different—something outstanding. She hates a commonplace existence. She told me last night that at last she saw a way to realize her ambition. Other women have climbed the Alps, she said, explored the Andes, and nosed into all sorts of queer places. She said that she had the strength and the courage to do as much as any woman can. And she thought her trip to the Valley of Arcana would make a good beginning. It really amounted to a lot, she said, for a girl to be the first, so far as anybody knows, to enter that hidden valley. It would add something to the geographical knowledge of the state, and who knew what she might not discover?

"I never before saw her so enthusiastic over anything. And now that she has come so far, I'd be the last one on earth to turn her back. So you must go on—you and Charmian and Andy and Marblehead. I can live here quite comfortably till you get back. I'm used to it—but I know now that I am too old to have considered coming along."

"Mary," said the doctor—and his unhandsome face was aglow with appreciation—"I am proud to know you. Your devotion to that girl is wonderful. But I think your present sacrifice is too great. Charmian will never—"

Mary Temple lifted a lean hand to stop him. "I won't have it any other way," she said. "To-morrow a couple of you men go back to the cache and pack in all that you can of the provisions we left there. That will give me an assurance of plenty, and you can start out, loaded to capacity again, from this point. I'll be all right. Don't worry about me. And what better plan have you to offer, anyway?"

"We could all camp here until you are fit to travel back," suggested Shonto, "and then—"

"Absolute nonsense!" Mary objected. "What's the use in wasting your opportunity that way? Don't try to be frivolously chivalrous, Doctor. This is no time for useless sentiment. Winter is close at hand, and this is a hard, hard country. It's time to look at the matter seriously."

"I'll go and talk with the others," said Shonto abruptly, and swung away up the cañon.

It was a difficult situation. No one wanted to leave a middle-aged woman alone in that wild cañon, with a vast, rugged wilderness between her and the comforts of life. But Mary remained tyrannically obdurate, so they decided that they would think the matter over during the two or three days which it would take Andy and Shirttail Henry to go for more provisions and return.

Early next morning the two set off on the back trail. The doctor busied himself at making a more or less permanent camp for Mary, provided they decided in the end to accept her ultimatum. Charmian spent hours at bringing her diary up to date. Mary, though in pain and obliged to move about with caution, feigned a limp and kept busy in order to deceive Charmian.

The afternoon of the third day of Henry and Andy's absence brought boredom to all three. The sky still was clear as crystal, with no suggestion of clouds; and down in the cañon it was warm while the sun remained overhead. Mary was confined to camp, of course, but she insisted that Charmian and Shonto go on a short trip of exploration either up or down the gorge.

The pair set off about two o'clock. The cañon floor was a mass of nigger-head boulders, through which snaked the rushing green creek. The walls were all but perpendicular in places and of a height close to two hundred and fifty feet. Few trees grew near the floor of the cañon, but there were numberless entanglements of driftwood from which to draw upon for fuel.

The birds were singing their praise of the comforting sunlight. Delicate ferns, unmolested by the frost, waved their green fronds above stones set in the cañon walls, their stems upreared from soft, vari-coloured mossbanks as lustrous and yielding as Oriental rugs and sparkling with diamonds of dew. A pensive languor pervaded the cañon, a sort of armistice between the mellow sun warmth and the gorge's lifelong heritage of clammy coldness. It made these human beings moody. The warmth was the gipsy warmth of early springtime, when the smells of earth are sweetest, as, deep down within the soil, the sleepy seeds begin to rub their eyes and stretch in their great awakening to a short life of ceaseless struggles. The pair were moody because they realized that it was not spring, that the half-hearted promise of the sun was altogether insincere. And while they were susceptible to the indolence of this tantalizing afternoon, the false warmth stirred their blood and kindled their imaginations to deeds of high emprise and thoughts of life as it ought to be, but never is. They were filled with vague feelings of unrest; they spoke but little and dreamed ambitious girlish and boyish dreams.

"Let's sit down," said Charmian, when they were a mile or more from camp.

An ancient bleached pine log had drifted into a little nook of rocks, where it was upheld from the floor by short, broken-off, horizontal limbs to a convenient height for a seat. It looked like a great white thousand-legged worm with porcupine quills in its back, said Charmian, as she seated herself between two of the upper-side stumps of limbs.

"What a day!" she continued. "I never was more ambitious in my life, Doctor, but I just want to sit here and ambish with my eyes half closed. I didn't know one could be lazy and ambitious at the same time. I imagine dope must affect one something like this. Gee, but I could slay pirates on the Spanish Main this afternoon—that is, if they'd move the Spanish Main up here to this log and I could keep from gaping long enough to draw my cutlass. Don't know that I'd want to kill pirates, either—I'd rather be a pirate myself and murder honest people. But either would be an effort—unless I could sit here and slay 'em with the evil eye."

She made an arm-rest of one of the stumpy branches and sank her round chin in one hand. The posture pushed up one ruddy cheek and caused her red lips to show a pout, and that odd little upward flirt at one corner lent them an unconscious smile. The long dark lashes, so delicately upturned at the end, drooped downward. Her profile stood out clean-cut against the flimsy light of the winter sun. Her throat showed soft and dimpled and dusky. Her hoard of hair had loosened and slipped downward in artistic disarray. She relaxed, eyes half closed, and her sinuous body slackened as it settled into unrestrained repose. Her full bosom rose and fell as softly and smoothly as the oily ground swell of a lazy tropic bay.

Inman Shonto likened womanly beauty to that of flowers. He knew lily girls and primrose girls, daisy girls and violet and pansy girls, even sunflower girls. But here was a rose girl—a great passionate American beauty rose, bold in colouring, strong and stanch, upright and unafraid, dominant, outstanding amid the other flowers, but owner of all the loveliness and grace of the lesser blossoms, as delicate of texture and as compelling in its tenderness.

The firm, puckered, rather thick lips of Dr. Shonto made a corrugated horizontal line as he drank in the beauty of the picture the drooping girl unconsciously posed for him. He thought of his own pale-blue eyes, his sparse sandy eyebrows, his thin, neutral-coloured hair, his pitted, Gargantuan nose. But he straightened. He had the body of a gladiator, the heart of a knight, the soul of a poet, and his intellect had brought both fame and wealth to his feet. The doctor knew all this; he knew himself, his possibilities and his limitations. He wanted this girl—he deserved her—he had given up his important work to go with her on this impulsively planned expedition and shield her and win her. She was a combination of all that he desired in a wife. To let Andy Jerome take her away from him would be an injustice to all concerned. His brains and his character and his manhood had made an appeal to her, he felt. Were these attributes enough for her? Was not he possessed of attributes of sufficient worthiness to offer in exchange for her beauty and womanly charm? And some women, he knew, were strangely attracted by an ugly man who offers them virility and a masterful personality. And nearly all such women, he had noted in his vast experience of life, were lovely women and intensely feminine.

"Charmian," he said suddenly, in a voice just loud enough to be heard above the boisterous laughter of the creek, "I've been thinking, since the night Andy and I first saw you at El Trono de Tolerancia, that maybe you're the woman I have been waiting for and longing for ever since I became a man. I came upon this trip with you to find out if my intuition had told me right. It has. The last week of you has shown me that you and I will not be doing our full duty to life unless we are together."

Her supple body tensed a trifle, then relaxed again. Her long lashes had lifted until he saw the silken sheen of her dark eyes, but now they were dropped once more.

"I'll admit that I have gone about this thing with practicality," he continued. "It is, perhaps, my scientific nature that caused me to. It's better that way. It's safest. Boys don't make love as I am making it, but I'm no boy, though I'm none the less sincere. I look upon successful marriage as the ideal partnership. And you will realize when you are a little older, as I do, that companionship is the most important feature of married life. Don't think that I don't love you. I do—deeply. But I'm not offering you the blind, fiery, uncontrolled passion of a youth in his twenties. I'm offering you the sincere love of a mature, reasoning man. What do you think of it?"

Charmian Reemy opened her eyes and stole a quick glance at him. The colour in her face was heightened only a little; and, though her heart may have beat a little faster, she was not greatly confused. But a feeling of triumph glowed warm within her. That she, by the not consciously exercised force of her personality and feminine charm, had intrigued this man of big achievements into a proposal of marriage was thrilling.

He was so desperately in earnest that his homely face was transfigured. Facial ugliness she saw only in the light of great strength. His broad smile was winning, tolerant, unutterably tender. His eyes were kind, whimsical, wistful; and there was in them now a lustre that she never had seen glowing there before.

Inman Shonto was not ugly now. The great soul of the man had enthroned itself in his countenance. The effect was spellbinding.

Charmian had told herself that, if ever she married again, she would marry a big man, a man of accomplishment. Her husband had been a big man in his small way. He had been a money-maker, a George F. Babbitt, but the girl-wife had not been able to interest herself in his activities. He had created nothing, discovered nothing, added nothing to the knowledge or welfare of the race. Walter J. Reemy had been commonplace in every way—a man whose commonplace mind followed a daily routine of commonplaceness.

"You and I, Charmian," the doctor was saying while she dreamed, "can make our life together an ideal one. Won't you even consider it?"

She had closed her eyes again, but now she opened them and smiled at him half bashfully.

"I am considering it," she said.

Shonto grasped her hand with eagerness and pressed it. "Thank heaven for that encouragement," he whispered fervently.

"But—but could I ever understand you?" asked Charmian. "I'm nothing—nobody—a dreamer. They say that I am pretty. If so, isn't it merely that which has attracted you to me, Doctor? If we were married, wouldn't you shut yourself away from me, treat me generously and courteously and devotedly, but at the same time never take me into your confidence? Don't you want me merely as an ornament for the mantle of your success?"

"Why should that be, Charmian?"

"Haven't you already declined to take me into your confidence about your work—about the glands? I didn't ask much, did I? I wasn't trying to pry into your secrets—the mysteries of your profession. I was just looking for a little enlightenment on a subject that has interested me ever since it was brought to the attention of the general public. And you shut up like a clam."

Shonto's face showed troubled lines.

"I tried to explain, very carefully," he pointed out, "that, in this instance, there is a peculiar reason why I cannot tell you what you want to know. But there may come a time when I shall feel at liberty to tell you all. Please trust me—and believe me when I say that, if you can look on my proposal in a favourable light, I will tell you everything. Don't you think me worthy of such trust, Charmian?"

There was a pleading note in his tones, though they were none the less manly, that caused her to say impulsively:

"Of course I trust you. I know you must have an excellent reason for not talking over your work with me. I'm afraid I'm pretty much of a kid at times, Doctor. And I'll—I'll— Well, I'll think about what you said. Oh, but what a matter-of-fact way we're taking to talk about such a subject! I think— My goodness! Here comes Andy—alone!"

CHAPTER XIV
THE LONG STRAW

ANDY JEROME came swinging down the cañon with the stride of a conquering hero, straight and strong under a burdensome pack. Both Charmian and Shonto regarded him in admiration as he came—he was so handsome, so well fortified with the confidence of youth, so sure that his vigorous young manhood was a match for any obstacle.

Charmian shouted and waved her hand. The homecomer waved back and sent the echoes cantering down the gorge after his long-drawn baritone whoop of greeting.

"What can have happened to Henry?" the young widow murmured, half to herself.

Shonto made no reply, but his face looked worried.

"Well, for mercy's sake!" cried the girl when Andy was close enough to hear her high-pitched words. "Where are you coming from? Where's the weather bureau?"

Andy Jerome came swinging on, slipping on the nigger-heads repeatedly, but always catching himself with the indifference that springy, always-ready muscles bequeath to youth.

"Some trip!" he laughed. "I just naturally walked old Marblehead off his feet. Then I left him to die and made the rounds alone."

He reached them, eased his pack to the stones with a great sigh, and held out both hands to them—his right to Charmian.

"Golly, I'm tired!" he ejaculated; but he looked as if any weariness that he might feel would forsake him after an hour's rest.

"Where *is* Henry?" asked Shonto soberly. "And how are you back so soon?—and coming down the gorge?"

"Well, last question answered first, I'm hitting her up down the gorge because I discovered an easier route back than the one Henry brought us over. And Henry is on his way home to write a letter to the Weather Bureau for a new rain gauge."

"Andy, you don't mean it!"—from Charmian Reemy.

"Sure do. I couldn't hold 'im. Thought I'd talked him out of shaking us, but in the night, while I was pounding my ear, he ups and beats it."

"But his money?" said Shonto.

"Oh, I paid him in advance," Charmian confessed with guilty reticence.

"The old rascal!" the doctor snorted.

"But I'm not worrying," Andy continued. "He'd virtually told me how to find the Valley of Arcana, and it strikes me that he's already about fulfilled his contract. I believe I can go straight to it from here. I'll tell you later what I got out of him.

"Personally, I won't miss the old coot in the least. He's not so much in the mountains. I walked the head off the old boy on the trip back to the cache. I let myself out—see?—which I couldn't do in travelling with you folks—if you'll pardon me. So I took our bold mountaineer on for a regular ramble, and I had him begging for less speed three hours out of camp."

"He's quite a little older than you are, Andy," Charmian made reminder.

She did not exactly approve of Andy's slightly boastful tone. Dr. Shonto caught the note in her voice, and hastened to say:

"Don't pay too much attention to our young friend's high opinion of his own prowess. Ordinarily Andy isn't the least bit boastful. But we're living a more or less primitive life these days. Our existence may depend on what we can do with our legs and arms and hands. Surmounting the difficulties of this wilderness has become the most important thing in our lives. We must excuse one another for being primevally proud of our little achievements."

"Good work, Doctor!" laughed Andy, a trifle red of face. "Was I shooting the old bazoo too hard? Maybe so. Thanks for your explanation to Charmian. The doctor's a wonder at keeping the serene equilibrium of camp life at par. He always understands that folks are different once they've shaken the dust of civilization from their feet. They're more primitive—that's right.

"Well, to continue, old Henry has been worrying ever since the bell burro made a sandwich out of his old gauge. Reading that gauge and sending in his reports are the greatest things in life for him. And so—well, he just up and hit the trail, that's all. He's got a loose screw in his head, of course. So we were camped at the cache, ready to start back in the morning. And when I found he'd gone I knew right away what had happened and struck out at dawn alone. And—boasting or no boasting—I've brought all that I meant to pack in and at least half of what Shirttail Henry had laid out for his pack. So we're not so bad off, after all. How's our pillar of determination and her sprain?"

The three walked down the cañon toward their camp, Shonto carrying the pack. Andy told the others, as they stumbled over the round, smooth stone cannon balls of the creek-bed, what Shirttail Henry had divulged concerning the onward trail to the Valley of Arcana.

When they had climbed the steep southern wall of the cañon in which they were encamped they would find themselves on a wooded plateau, none too level. For several miles they would travel across timberland, then the trees would become scarcer and patches of chaparral would make their appearance. Gradually the chaparral would claim the land, and would extend for miles—how many he did not know—to the country immediately surrounding the valley of their quest. Halfway through this immense stretch of prickly brush Reed, the ranger, and his companions had been obliged to discontinue the trip.

"But they always tried it in summer," said Andy. "In summer or spring, when the air is hot and a fellow needs a lot of water. It's cool now—cold—and we won't suffer much along that line. We'll pack every drop of water we can and nurse it religiously. We won't need much. Strikes me a fellow could catch enough dew over night to last him all next day. Stretch out a closely woven piece of canvas, maybe. And if it should rain or snow, we'd perhaps be mighty uncomfortable, but we'd be assured of plenty of water."

"Let's not pray for either," the girl suggested. "I'd rather chance a drought."

"For my part," said Shonto, "I almost wish we could go back and give it up entirely. It's going to be serious if winter overtakes us; and, because of the many delays we've been up against, it strikes me that that's almost sure to happen."

"Can't give up and go back now, with Mary unable to travel," Andy reminded him.

"Yes, that's so," sighed the older man. "We're in for it now, and we may as well forge on as to twiddle our thumbs in the cañon while Mary's—er—sprain gets better. But I'll tell you one thing: I'm never going to consent to leave that woman alone in the gorge, crippled as she is. Either you or I, Andy, must stay with her. Of course Charmian must go on, if anybody does; this is her circus. And as you are the expert mountaineer of the party, I have decided to stay with Mary. But it's going to give me grey hairs whether I go or stay. If I go, Mary will be constantly on my guilty mind. If I stay with her, I won't be able to sleep for worrying about you two."

"Shucks, Doctor! You're not like yourself at all here lately," was Andy's complaint. "You used to be a sport—nothing was too rough for you."

"I never had a couple of women along with me before," Shonto defended himself. "And I don't know that I've ever before been in quite so precarious a situation, Andy. It's no difficult matter to become food for the coyotes in a country like we're in."

All three were a trifle serious now and talked but little. Charmian and Andy agreed with Dr. Shonto, however, that it would be ungenerous to leave Mary Temple alone in this dismal gorge while they continued the adventure. Andy had made no offer to stay and allow his friend to go with Charmian. His heart was leaping madly at thought of braving the trail into an unknown land with her alone.

Mary Temple listened without a show of consternation to the story of Shirttail Henry's duty-bound flight.

"Well," she observed dispassionately, "we seem destined to lose our support. First the Morleys and Leach threw us down, and now the good ship *Marblehead* goes on the rocks. He was more or less of a doodunk, anyway."

"What's a doodunk?" Andy asked.

"A doodunk," she informed her questioner, "is something that makes a man say damn and a woman think damn. For example, a doodunk is a lumpy place in a mattress. But Henry's going knocks something galley west and crooked."

"What's that?" Charmian wished to know.

"With Henry out of it, who's going to be the madman that leans over you and chokes you in the Valley of Arcana?" snapped Mary. "I hope you haven't forgotten that, Charmian Reemy! You wait! Madame Destrehan knows—she saw it all!"

Mary was not exactly in an amiable mood, but the others broached the subject of some one remaining with her, nevertheless. To their utter surprise, she made reply:

"Well, I've been thinking that over myself this afternoon. I guess maybe you're right, at that. Charmian must go on—that's settled. This is her fool party, and the rest of us are just invited guests. So either Doctor Shonto or Andy will have to stay with me, and the other one go on with Charmian and get the ridiculous thing over with while my ankle's getting well."

"Now, neither of you two fellows want to stay with an old battleaxe like me. I know that. Just the same, all alone here in this cold, dark cañon this afternoon, I changed my tune. So you'll draw straws to see which one is elected. And as I'm the innocent party concerned, I'll hold the straws. Suit you?"

Her defiant eyes coasted from Shonto to the younger man.

"Certainly," both made answer. And Andy added, in tones none too strong:

"Nothing could be fairer."

"All right." Mary bent over—with difficulty and pain, the doctor noted—and took up from the ground a box of safety matches. She extracted two, closed the box and dropped it, and turned herself slowly on her rocky throne until her back was toward the expectant gamblers. "Got a piece of money, either of you?" she asked.

Andy produced a silver coin.

"Toss it up," commanded the arbiter of their fortunes. "Heads, the doctor draws first; tails, Andy gets first crack. And the one that draws the long match stays with me. What about it?"

"Suits me," both men said; and Andy flipped the half-dollar into the air.

"Tails," he announced as the coin rang on the stones. "I draw first."

Mary wheeled slowly back and faced them. She held out one big-veined and skinny hand, above the closed fingers of which two match-heads protruded.

With a swift glance at his rival, Andy took a step and stood before her, hesitated a moment, then reached out and pulled a match.

He caught his breath, turned red, and glanced confusedly at Charmian.

He had drawn an entire match—the long straw. He was elected to stay with Mary Temple.

"I don't care if I did cheat," Mary consoled herself as she sought her bed early that night. "They'll never guess that neither match was broken. Andy had no chance to win—and I wanted it that way."

But at the same time that she was saying this Dr. Shonto sat alone over the red coals of the dying campfire. Charmian and Andy were strolling down the cañon together under the light of the moon, and the girl did not protest when Andy's arm stole round her waist.

CHAPTER XV
VAGRANCY CAÑON

"CHARMIAN," said Andy passionately, "do you know that I love you more than anything else in all the world? I can't live without you, darling! Don't want to live without you! You know I love you, don't you, dear? Tell me you know it! You must know it! You can't help but know! I've loved you from the moment I first set eyes on you, when you stood in the door in your evening gown at El Trono de Tolerancia. God, how I love you, Charmian!"

He stopped her, made her face him, and threw his other arm about her. He was trembling violently, and in the moonlight she saw the twitching of his parted lips.

"Charmian! Charmian!" he cried brokenly, as he realized that she was not struggling in his arms. "You love me, don't you? I know you love me! God!"

He tightened his hold on her, drew her close to his breast, kissed her dark hair, then savagely threw her body sidewise and found her lips with his.

She was shaken—swept away. He was so young, so handsome, so strong, so intensely masculine. Every primitive instinct of her being went out to him. She could no more escape the passionate appeal of the male in him than can the innocent, nature-ruled females of the wilderness escape at mating time. She had no desire to escape. They were man and woman, alone under the stars and the moon, in a deep, grim cañon that scarred the heart of this wild region; and all the sounding brass and tinkling cymbals of our false and hectic civilization were far away. A man and a woman, alone and aloof as Adam and Eve in the Garden of Eden, young, courageous, ripe for love. "Male and female created he them." She gave him her warm, firm lips. He kissed her lips and eyes and her dusky throat, while the blood hammered in his veins as if freshets of old port wine were rushing through them.

They spoke a thousand words that night, reclining in each other's arms on the uncompromising floor of that severe old gorge, but they only said, "I love you." They said it in a hundred ways, lips to lips, but no way was original. Love knows no originality when it is sincere. "I love you" is all that can be said—three words, "I love you," but they are the hinges that swing the door of life.

"And to-morrow you're going with him to the Valley of Arcana, Charmian! Will you think of me all the time, dearest? You won't listen if he makes love to you, will you, Charmian? I know you won't—you're the dearest, truest, sweetest girl on earth! Oh, why did I have to draw the long match! Why couldn't I go with you instead of him? But as soon as you find the valley, you'll come right back, won't you, honey?"

"Of course"—and she smothered the words against his lips.

"I wonder, if I were to tell him that we love each other, if he wouldn't consent to let me go instead. If Mary needs help, he, being a doctor, ought to stay with her. But then I couldn't ask it. He wouldn't expect me to. I know he'd give in to me—but he'd think I wasn't a sport. We've always played square—the doctor and I. I hope he doesn't love you too much, Charmian. Has he told you that he loves you? What were you saying in the cañon this afternoon?"

"He told me he loved me," said Charmian softly.

"He did!"—belligerently. "And what—what did you say?"

"I—I promised to consider it, Andy. I couldn't think of anything else to say. And that was before you—before to-night, you know."

"Why didn't you tell him there was nothing doing?"

"I couldn't. I didn't want to— That is, I—I—he took me so by surprise. And you hadn't once mentioned love to me then, Andy. And who could hurt his feelings—he's such a dear—such a manly man!"

"But you knew I was going to blurt it out sometime—when I found my nerve."

"I know—I felt it, I guess. But—oh, don't think of Doctor Shonto to-night. I love you—I love *you*! I don't want to think of anything else in all the world!"

The hour was late when they returned to camp, floating in air. The doctor had long since sought his blankets. They lengthened the good-night kiss of their new-found love, for in the morning there would be no opportunity to kiss before the parting.

Charmian, Andy, and Shonto had talked at length over the directions given to Andy by the defaulting Henry for the continuation of the journey. Before the girl and Andy had gone down the gorge for their love-making all arrangements had been made for an early-morning start.

The four were rather silent as they ate breakfast in the frosty cañon. Mary Temple assumed the initiative in such conversation as was indulged in, fussing over the out-going pair, as needlessly agitated as a mother hen, a couple of whose brood are ducklings and persist in taking to the water. But at last the meal was over, the good-byes were spoken, the packs and water-bags shouldered, the final love message wirelessed between Charmian and Andy. And now Mary stood needlessly shading her eyes with her hand as she watched the couple up the gorge, so dismal at that early-morning hour, while Andy watched from a seat on a large boulder, spread-legged, with hands clasped between his knees, hopelessness in his eyes.

Then shrilly shouted the mother hen after her erring ducklings:

"Doctor! *Doc*-tor! Did you leave Andy plenty of his little pills?"

Poor Mary Temple! She was not gifted with the ability to look into the future for which she gave Madame Destrehan credit. Had she been able to she could have envisioned Dr. Shonto trudging wearily back to her and Andy six days later—alone.

Half a mile up the clammy cañon from the camp Charmian and the doctor turned abruptly to the right and entered a steep branch cañon that tentacled from the larger one to the south. Their course was still due south, according to the bewhiskered deserter, and, as they carried a dependable compass, it was without misgivings that they abandoned landmarks which they knew and clambered upward into an unknown country.

The branch cañon was rock-tenoned and perilously steep, though mercifully dry for a mile above its mouth. It was, said Charmian, the most outspoken cañon in its querulous complaints over their trespassing that they had as yet encountered. It seemed that nature had designed it as the closest attempt to an impossible approach to what was beyond as lay within her power. Into its V bottom she had in a fit of anger hurled immense boulders from the heights above. She had uptilted in her tantrum huge strata of leaflike stone whose edges were sharp as a butcher's cleaver. Then, out to make a night of it, she had poured rubble from the size of an egg to that of a muskmelon down the reaching slopes, wildly mirthful as a miser raining his shekels from bags to glittering heaps on the table-top. These rubble slides were sometimes half a mile in length—nothing but a slanted sea of round, smooth stones of reddish hue, with not a grain of soil or one single gasping blade of vegetation. Across these slides the wanderers laboured heavily, for the stones, always eager to continue their interrupted rush into the cañon, gave under their feet like dough; often slid under them, carrying them along on the crest of a new slide; and, thus releasing the pressure, caused slides above them which threatened to swoop down and engulf them or mangle their arms and legs; threw them headlong on occasion; twisted their ankles; endangered every bone; made progress a nightmare of apprehensions by clutching their feet at every step, as when the dream-tortured victim tries to flee from some murderous phantom and terror palsies his legs. Once Shonto pitched headlong as the rubble sank under his feet like breaking ice. The break started a slide above him, which extended upward and upward to the lip of the cañon until their ears were filled with the deafening roar of a far-reaching avalanche. Large stones were pushed upward above the mass, and, released, came bounding down alone over the top of the sliding sea, gaining momentum at every leap, living devils of menace.

For a brief space the two were bewildered, the doctor the more so because his head had struck a rock in falling and left him dazed. Then Charmian screamed, and he struggled up and ploughed a way to her side. Almost before they could plan escape the vanguard of the great slide was rushing past them and piling up about their ankles.

"The other side!" shouted the doctor.

He grasped her hand and together they plunged recklessly toward the V bottom of the cañon. It was no longer dry, and this feature had forced them to traverse the rubble, for the opposite wall was all but perpendicular, with overhanging crags. There was no footing. Every frantic step landed them on top of a rolling stone or in the midst of a nest of them. Their ankles turned; they were pitched drunkenly from right to left, thrown to their knees, carried downward in a sitting posture, sometimes backward. The increasing roar was terrifying; a tidal wave of reddish stones was vomited at them—a charging army pursuing them, its skirmish line already heckling them, its cannon balls pounding down from the artillery in the rear.

Charmian pitched forward; would have sprawled on her face upon the wriggling mass of stones had the doctor lost his crushing grip on her hand. Her right arm was almost jerked from its socket as their arms straightened between them and the doctor held on. She thought of her girlhood game of "crack the whip," when she had been the "snapper" at the tail end of the line and had absorbed the greatest part of the dizzying shock. Next moment she felt herself swept up into his arms, pack and all; and then—though only Heaven knows how he did it—the man pitched with his burden into the cañon, lunged through the water, and started to climb the wall on the opposite side.

Here she struggled free. "I'm all right," she panted. "I can climb. Oh, hurry!"

Upwards they struggled, grasping jutting stones and the roots of bushes. Into the cañon below them poured the avalanche of stones with the clatter of a billion dice. They struggled on for fifty feet or more, then the girl dropped in helpless exhaustion; and Shonto, faring little better, threw himself down beside her.

"We're safe," he gulped. "Just—just rest."

Gradually the roar subsided while they lay there gasping for the air that seemed to be denied them. Only an occasional angry snarl came from some section of the slide that tried to renew the wild dervish dance of destruction. Then all sounds ceased, and the beleaguered travellers sat up and gazed at the opposite side of the cañon. Everything looked as it had looked before the doctor fell, except that the bottom of the cañon was covered with rubble to a depth of maybe twenty feet. The freshets of a hundred springs to come would carry these on down towards the floor of the mother cañon below, and all would seem to be as it had been for centuries past until some leaping deer or prowling cougar or skulking coyote passed that way and started another slide.

"Gosh!" breathed Charmian. "Ain't nature wonderful! Thanks for the lift, dear old thing. Well, who's scared? Where do we go from here?"

"That's the difficulty," said Shonto seriously. "I don't like to risk another slide by travelling over the rubble stones again, and if we keep to this side of the cañon we won't make half a mile an hour. And to walk up the floor of the cañon means wet feet and a continual battle with big boulders and outcroppings."

But time was of the essence of their contract. They risked the slides again.

They crossed two more as large as the one on which catastrophe had threatened, then several of lesser dimensions until they went out of the district of slides. Now they worked their slow way along the same steep slope, over roots and rocks and soft black soil, mellow with decayed chaparral leaves and foamy from the heaving frost. The travelling was heart-breaking until they stepped into a deer trail by sheerest accident. Birds cheered them along their way—silent, solemn birds, but companionable in their flattering curiosity. They were very small birds with indistinguishable necks, impossible long bills, big heads, swollen breasts, dull colouring, and manners pontifical in seriousness. These were the questioning little aborigines that, on the other side of the divide, Mary Temple had called squirks, explaining that a squirk was an important little man who looked like a shabbily clothed preacher, but who made his living by taking orders for enlargements of portrait photographs.

The cañon dwindled—petered out entirely on the ample breast of a hill. It that had been so jagged and yawning and formidable down below now showed no cause for its being—Vagrancy Cañon, Charmian named it because, she said, it could show no visible means of support. Over the rounded breast of the eminence they trailed and found themselves on virtually level land, on the wooded plateau of Shirttail Henry's promise. The day was almost spent; they retraced their way back to the cañon, to where they had seen a spring. Fleecy clouds drifted across the sky, mobilizing in the west, where the reflection of the sinking sun on the far-off ocean was re-reflected on their snowy scallops—orange, cerise, and giddy yellow.

They camped by the little spring.

CHAPTER XVI
THE CAMP IN VAGRANCY CAÑON

SHONTO collected wood and built a fire, while Charmian undid the packs. At an early hour the sun sank behind the mountain peaks, and night descended fast. They cooked and ate a simple meal and wasted not a crumb, for this was a serious business that they were upon and the success of it might depend on their husbanding of food.

They cleaned up after the meal, and, while the thin light lasted, sought out their sleeping places for the night and spread the blankets. Both were ineffably weary, for even Charmian's pack was a heavy one. But the warmth of the leaping fire that they now built up from the red cooking coals soothed their aching joints and muscles and made existence rosier. They sat one on either side of it, and Shonto rolled and lighted a cigarette to be drawn upon between sips of hot black coffee.

"I'll take one too, please," said Charmian. "I don't often smoke, but I know how; and it seems to me that, with only us two away out here in the land of nowhere, I ought to smoke to keep you company. Do you approve of women smoking, Doctor?"

"Never before having had any women to be solicitous about," replied Shonto thoughtfully, as he rolled her cigarette, "I have never given the subject much thought."

He arose and handed her the rolled cylinder. She accepted it a bit awkwardly and ran the tip of her pink tongue along the edge of the paper to moisten it. With the toe of his heavy high-laced boot he scraped a burning twig from the fire and supplied her with a light.

"Women who smoke not being looked upon with favour," he remarked, as he squatted over his coffee cup again, "strikes me as only another example of the slavery to which woman has been subjected from the beginning of history. Laying aside any harm that may come from the practice, why shouldn't she smoke? It may stain her teeth and work havoc with her digestive apparatus, but her teeth and digestive apparatus are identical with man's. So we can't justly prohibit her from smoking on those grounds. The smoking woman is looked upon with disfavour, then, merely because tradition has it that she cannot smoke and remain in the good graces of conservative society. To the bourgeois mind, she is not a lady. Now, the act of smoking is in itself absolutely no more unmoral than spinning a top. If men derived pleasure from top-spinning, doubtless women would be permitted to likewise enjoy themselves. Men eat candy, and women may do so too without losing caste. Just why they can't smoke without getting in bad is beyond me."

"It's simply another of our stupid taboos," said Charmian, puffing grandly to show her independence, and choking just a little now and then. "We're hemmed in with taboos on all sides. They are grounded in our conservative minds from childhood, and we can't shake them off. Years ago some one decided that women ought not to smoke. Some one agreed with him. Others took it up, perhaps; and finally it became the accepted rule. So in childhood we were taught that women shouldn't smoke—that good women didn't smoke. We grew up unaccustomed to see women smoking. Therefore when we encountered an occasional individual who did smoke, she was considered immoral. But why immoral? What is there immoral about placing a cigarette between one's lips, lighting it, and inhaling and exhaling the smoke? Injurious it may be, but we're not discussing that phase of the subject. A man may thus injure himself with impunity, but if a woman does so she is immoral. Now isn't that illogical?"

"Logic plays a small part in our lives," said Shonto. "We're not on very friendly terms with logic. Logic means thinking and shaking off the old ideas that are handed down to us from the ancients, and we're too lazy to do that. Logic calls for reasoning, and why reason when our beliefs and our behaviour have been regulated for us for seventeen or eighteen hundred years? Why think for ourselves, when the ancients went to so much trouble to prescribe for us our taboos and our religious beliefs and our standard of morals? Why think, in short? It's such hard work. And it has a tendency to uproot old beliefs in which we are quite comfortable. We might feel the urge to clean house if we sat down and thought a little, and everybody knows how upsetting is house-cleaning day!"

"And isn't there any hope for us, Doctor Shonto? Will nothing make us think?"

Shonto's dull eyes brightened. "Yes, we're beginning to think. The great war did that much for us here in America, anyway. I really believe there is a serious attempt being made to-day to think. People are at least trying to think. They are at least reading more thoughtful books than ever before, and, thank God, we have a few men who are capable of writing thoughtful books! There's a whisper going along the line, a faint and timorous suggestion that maybe all is not as it should be on this earth—that maybe we are selling our heritage for a mess of pottage—that perhaps we are trampling life's riches under our feet, like swine trampling into the mud nuggets of gold as they rush to the swill trough.

"But as yet only the people who have been trying for some time to think are absorbing the books which will help them to think. These books are beyond the masses. The authors of many of them are slaves to style and big-sounding words. The newspapers are the unthinking man's school—and what a farce, what a seedbed of corruption they are! Reporters and editors must remain loyal to the policies of their papers, regardless of their own opinions. They who could help us to think are forbidden to do so on the penalty of losing their jobs.

"And the children of this country, and doubtless every other so-called civilized country, must depend upon the schools to learn to think. And every thinking teacher who takes the rostrum is fired for his attempt to break down the walls of superstition and slash the hedges of tradition. But for all that, the youth of this country at least are gradually—no, pretty swiftly—breaking away. The world-old conflict between Age and Youth is at its hottest now. In the past thirty years the world has made revolutionary discoveries which are daily changing our lives and methods of thinking. All this came about after Age had settled down to an acceptance of life without any changes. At forty or fifty one does not readily change his views. The sutures of his skull are closed, and it is difficult for him to learn new ideas. He is beyond the plastic period, and his head is as hard as his arteries. He is entirely unable to accept the electron theory in the place of 'in six days the Lord made heaven and earth, the sea, and all that in them is.' Simply because he never heard of the electron theory at the age when his brain was capable of accepting a new idea. It's too late for him—he's hopeless. But he's dying off! To-morrow he won't be running the world. His sons and his daughters will be in the saddle.

"And they have come upon the earth and grown to young manhood and young womanhood while these radical changes were taking place. They are able to consider, even accept, the findings of modern science because they are presented to them while their brains are still in the receptive period of life. What seems most plausible to them they accept, and they naturally will laugh at the old traditions, superstitions, taboos, and beliefs that have come down to us from the days of savagery, and which were ingrained in the lives of their parents when *they* were of a receptive age. Fifty years, I think, will show many a mossy institution crumbled to ashes. The Aged of to-day will be gone, without having been able to force their lifelong beliefs on Youth. Then Youth will become Old Age, and if we have progressed at all, the coming generation will refuse to accept what *their* fathers and mothers believed in and made the ruling factor in their lives. So the conflict between Age and Youth, between conservatism and change, between receptive minds and locked minds, goes on to the end of time."

"My stars!" cried Charmian. "You're more pessimistic about it—more hopeless—than I am, even!"

"I hadn't finished," said Shonto dreamily. "That will be the result unless men learn to think. They have brains, why don't they think? Because they have been relieved of the necessity for thinking by the ancient spellbinders whom we still worship to-day. That's why they don't think. Man is naturally lazy—more so mentally than any other way. If others have done his thinking for him, he should worry! It gives him time to pursue the things that he likes—money, pleasure, love, self-aggrandizement."

"Well, I understand all that. But it doesn't help."

"We're going to make him think in spite of himself," said Shonto. "We're going to give him a quicker brain, so that he will be compelled to think willy-nilly. His brain is good, but it needs exercise. And he has not been obliged to exercise it. Hence it has become slothful. Considering the progress that our few thinkers have made, the brain of the average man is far below normal. We must bring it up to normal so that it will exercise itself and grow whether he wants it to or not. Then he'll shed his stupidity and open his eyes, and maybe something will go bust in the wheels of the system that rules us. We're going to feed him the extract of the thyroid glands of sheep, sharpen his intellect, put the zip of life into him. Then he'll think, and he'll probably get mad. But we are only at the beginning of this great study of the glands and their secretions, and what they may do for man.

"The thyroid is the gland of energy. It controls the growth of certain organs and tissues of brain and sex. The internal secretions of our thyroid glands, mind you, are not necessary to life. If these secretions are inadequate, we may go on living, but we shall be below normal mentally, and our level of energy will remain low. But when more thyroid is introduced into the system our vital chemical reactions will speed up. It has been proved and accepted without qualification by men of science that the more thyroid a person has the more energetic will he be. Our dull people are, in many cases, only victims of an insufficiency of thyroid. One's memory is affected by his thyroid glands. And without memory, who can learn? Judgment depends on memory, doesn't it? It requires memory, the association of experiences. Quick thinking calls for thyroid glands that are normal. Do you know, Charmian, that many criminals are only the victims of their glands—and that science can probably correct this in time by supplying the unfortunates with the gland secretions which they lack? Do you realize that it is, even now, an established scientific fact that idiocy can be cured by feeding the subject the extract of the thyroid glands of sheep? And—and— Well, I simply have great hopes for the race if science eventually finds it possible to quicken the thinking apparatus by the introduction of gland extracts."

"Has anything been accomplished along that line?" she asked. "Have you accomplished anything?"

"I have," he told her. "I am convinced that we are on the right track."

"Tell me of some case," she begged.

He seemed to be searching his mind. "The greater part of the cases that I have handled," he said at last, "were concerned with subjects whose maladies I cannot discuss with you because of their delicate nature. In brief, subjects who were troubled with the problems of sex. And such cases as I have had that called for the introduction of thyroxin are still in the experimental stage. Only time will tell whether we are right or not."

"But can't you notice results?"

"Oh, yes—in many cases. But whether or not the results will be permanent no one can say at present."

"For a little," she said thoughtfully, "I imagined you were about to tell me something, but you're still reticent and I shan't press you. Well, here we are, all alone together, on the outskirts of nowhere, and between us we have solved many riddles of the race. And I have been immoral and smoked a cigarette, if I wasn't immoral in the first place in coming here with you. But it seemed that in no other way could I find the Valley of Arcana—and here I am. I wonder if we're to begin crawling to victory to-morrow?"

"I don't like those clouds that we saw at sunset," he remarked. "But they're all gone now. The sky's as clear as ever."

Charmian gaped, placed a slim hand over her distorted mouth, and patted the aperture, ending with a burst of air that was wrenched out of her until her jaw muscles seemed to creak.

"Pardon me," she laughed. "I couldn't help it—I'm about all in. That means the blankets for mine. Good night, Doctor.

"How you have interested me," she sighed, as she rose to her feet and stretched her arms and torso as unreservedly as a young panther would. "You have worked so much—have accomplished so much. You make me feel like a baseball fan in the grandstand, yelling his head off over the good work of some famous player in the field. I hate fans. They're so willing to get entertainment from the achievements of others. They dote on baseball, know all the players by name and their records from A to Z. They never miss a game, never fail to bloat their blood vessels by shouting their approval. Yet not one of them can toss a rubber ball twenty feet in air and be sure of catching it!

"I'm not picking on baseball fans in particular. I just used them as a handy example. All of us in this world but the thinkers are fans. We're wild about the conveniences that electricity has brought to us, but not one out of a hundred of us could splice a broken electric wire. We rave over a famous lecturer or writer, but how many of us try to become lecturers or writers? Can you imagine a man—I know him—who never misses a professional billiard game, knows all the professional players, all the niceties of their work, but never takes a billiard cue in hand?

"Most of us are fans—we admire and worship and gloat over the success of the few, particularly if it is designed for our entertainment, but never make an effort at being anything ourselves. Oh, I'm sick of shouting from the grandstand, Doctor! I want to do something. I want to be one of the few who make the world go round for the others!"

"Leave the grandstand, then," said the doctor softly, "and come down on the diamond with me."

Charmian caught her breath at the suddenness of it. She had not suspected that she was leading herself into a trap. And she had given herself to Andy! She had let him fondle her, had told him that she loved him, with her lips pressed to his.

"I—I haven't finished thinking about it," she said hurriedly, and hastened off to her blankets.

For an hour she lay looking up at the black sky and the tracery of pine branches against it, thinking, thinking, groping patiently but fruitlessly.

Next morning at an early hour they climbed the hill again, crossed the wooded plateau, came upon the thinning trees and the encroaching brush. That afternoon they left all traces of the forest behind them, and faced a desolate sweep of chaparral, stretching away as far as the eye could see, hemmed in on the south by snowy peaks barely outlined against the paleness of the sky. And somewhere in the midst of that seemingly unbroken sea of hoary grey and antique gold the undiscovered Valley of Arcana lay in hiding.

CHAPTER XVII
BEAR PASS

YEARS beyond conjecture had passed since a great forest fire had swept across the waste of chaparral which Charmian and Doctor Shonto looked upon. Probably never before or since in the history of the California forests had such a far-reaching fire ravaged the peaks and valleys.

A mighty forest had stood there then, to be laid low by the consuming flames. In its place had come the comparatively rapid growing chaparral, claiming the land to the exclusion of all other vegetation. Here and there a lone pine stood erect and disdainful above the twelve-foot brush, and here and there on the ground under the bushes lay down trees, ancient corpses that had disintegrated to corklike particles and powder, mere shadows of logs that were ready to crumble when a boot toe touched them.

The chaparral was compromised of buckthorn bushes, interspersed with manzanita. The buckthorn bushes formed what is known as locked chaparral—which means that their prickly upper branches are twined and intertwined until they form a solid mat, more impenetrable than a hedge. So compact was this mat that little sun trickled through to the earth, and as a consequence of this not a blade of grass could live under the dense canopy. But even where a single chaparral bush grows in the open no grass will be found within a radius of ten feet on all sides of it. It claims the land, selfishly sucks all the nutriment from the soil, and will share existence with no other plant.

The ground under the canopy was covered with the tiny leaves that had shattered off through countless years. This carpet was several inches thick, with dry, newly shattered leaves on top, and, below these, leaves in various stages of disintegration, down to the bottom layer of powdered leaf-mould. To stand erect and try to push one's way into this thicket would be as useless as attempting to forge through a barbed-wire entanglement. But underneath the branches the ground was clean, and no limbs grew from the sturdy trunks of the bushes lower than a foot from the earth. And as the limbs had a decided upward trend, like the limbs of a cypress tree, there was ample opportunity for one to crawl on hands and knees for any distance that he might choose. Of course now and then close-growing bushes would balk him, but there always would be a way around. To travel through the thicket depended entirely on one's powers of endurance in reverting to the mode of going calling employed by his simian precursors. To hack a trail through was a task for an army of axemen.

The pilgrims seated themselves on the ground and looked expectantly at each other.

"What do you think of it, Doctor?" asked Charmian.

"I think," replied Shonto, "that we'd better go back."

"Honestly?"

"Honestly."

For a long time Charmian was thoughtful, a little pucker between her eyebrows. Then she resolutely shook her head, and her upper lip turned up a trifle in her characteristic smile.

"No, we've set our hands to the plough," she said. "'Go back' is not in my lexicon."

"I think," Shonto returned, "that a half-hour or so of crawling on all fours under that tangle of branches will convince the two of us that we've never known fatigue before."

"Which doesn't mean that you're not game, of course."

"I am thinking more of you than of myself," he told her.

"Don't do that," she requested. "I think I've shown that I'm pretty tough. And I'm of the opinion, Doctor, that I shall crawl better than you will. I have less weight to push along, and I'm somewhat of a tumbler, though I guess I've never told you. I can turn handsprings, do the cartwheel, and throw flip-flops forward and backward. My life has not been entirely wasted, you see. Besides all that, women are more primitive than men, both mentally and physically. I imagine that, 'way back in the misty ages when we were learning to pick up a club to defend ourselves instead of biting altogether, man was walking erect a long time before the female of the species stood up and tried the new fad. Don't you know that a woman can sit down on the floor with more comfort than a man? You birds are over-civilized, and that's what's the matter with the world. Are you ready? Let's go!"

In an hour Dr. Inman Shonto was ready to admit that her logic was sound. "You go back farther than primitive man," he puffed, as he lumbered along after her. "You go back to when we were saurians wallowing in the slime and the seaweed. You're a lizard."

In the beginning he had taken the lead, but his slow, clumsy progress had nettled her.

"Give me the compass," she had demanded. "I'll go ahead and show you how. It's a pity you're so big. 'The race is not to the swift, nor the battle to the strong'—Ecclesiastes something or other. They're to the springy-boned and wiggly. Watch auntie, Inman!"

Watching auntie was difficult, for auntie glided along so bonelessly and snakily that half the time she was out of sight and had to wait for him to catch up. When an occasional low-growing limb fought her demand for the right of way, she went flat and swam under it, while the man was obliged to surrender and find a way around it.

Often the packs on their shoulders caught like Absalom's hair, and then there was difficulty for both. One usually had to extricate the other. "You're like a pig caught under a fence," the widow told her companion. "Why don't you squeal when I pull your leg? And, my stars, you're heavy, man!"

Despite the carpet of leaves under them, their knees became chafed. They cut pieces of leather from the uppers of their high-laced boots, made two holes on either side of them, and tied them over their knees with heavy twine. Every muscle in their bodies ached. They were obliged to rest frequently, especially the doctor, to lie flat on the earth and straighten their limbs. At rare intervals they came upon breaks in the thicket, where for maybe several hundred feet they could walk erect. In one of these breaks, where two Digger pines grew, they made camp for their first night in the chaparral.

They were in the thicket another day and night and until noon of the next day. They had come upon deep cañons, where the chaparral broke and scrub oak grew. Here they found moisture, enough to replenish the water-bags, the contents of which they had been nursing carefully. But always the chaparral reached out to meet them when they had crossed one of these earth scars, and before long they were crawling again.

Toward noon of the third day they found themselves crawling over level land, where the ragged growth was sparse. Both were nearly spent, when of a sudden the land began descending rapidly. And almost before they were aware of it they were gazing down spellbound into an abyss which could be nothing else than the long-sought Valley of Arcana.

It was freakish. Neither had ever seen its like before. Thinking themselves in the midst of a waste of chaparral and far from their goal, the land suddenly had dropped to a shelf a thousand feet below them. Charmian said that, if she had had her eyes shut, she probably would have crawled right over the precipice and pitched to her death on the rocks below.

It was a miniature Grand Cañon of the Colorado, with surrounding walls as steep and perilous. The break was as abrupt and stupefying as the far-famed Pali of the Island of Oahu.

Far below them flashed a river, jade-green, a winding snake. Trees followed its course, and beyond were delectable meadows, half green, half brown in tinge. The spreading trees—probably live oaks—looked miniature, like buckthorn bushes; the lofty pines like toothpicks. Over crags below them eagles soared. Not a sound came; a vast, solemn hush hung over the smiling valley. In the far distance, perhaps seven or eight miles away, the saw-tooth tops of the craggy peaks that guarded the southern limit of the Valley of Arcana were dimly traced against the skim-milk blue of the sky. Below the peaks lay an enchanted lake, blue and sparkling, swimming miragelike in the sunlight.

For minutes neither of the trespassers spoke. Shonto stepped close to Charmian and took her hand, and side by side they gazed upon the wonders spread before them. They were awed by the grandeur and solemnity of this masterpiece of Nature, a little lonely, a little timid.

They had accomplished much. Probably never before in the annals of exploration had any one been forced to blaze a trail into an unknown country crawling on all fours. They were painfully weary and sore from the unaccustomed strain; their provisions were low, and but several mouthfuls of water remained in the canvas bags. But they had found the Valley of Arcana, and its myriad delights rewarded them for the torture they had undergone.

It was Charmian Reemy who broke the silence. "I think," she said, "that Ranger Reed was nearer to the Valley of Arcana than he knew when he turned back, discouraged. In an hour, Doctor, *we* might have turned back, too, with our grub and water so low."

They seated themselves on stones to discuss the situation.

It would be absolutely necessary for them to find a route down into the valley to replenish the water-bags. Also, they must have more food. They had lived principally on jerked venison for that day and the day before, conserving the other supplies, and had nibbled the strong nutritious chocolate from the army emergency rations which they carried. They had not dared to make coffee because they could not spare the water. The only firearm that they had brought along was the doctor's .22 rifle, because of its lightness. Shonto was a crack shot with the little weapon, and Charmian was obliged to shelve her repugnance for the slaughter of the innocents and give him permission to kill jackrabbits or any other small game that they might see.

These things decided, they nibbled a cake of chocolate each and divided the remaining "jerky" between them. They drank the last of the water. Then they set off along the lip of the precipice in search of a possible way to get down into the valley. After a mile or more of winding in and out among the outcroppings, boulders, and tentacles of chaparral that extended from the main thicket to the edge of the declivity they were seriously wondering whether it was possible to reach the floor of the valley at all. For the wall below them was, figuratively speaking, as perpendicular as the side of a skyscraper. They discovered several false breaks that promised to open upon routes leading downward, but each time they were halted by a yawning precipice as steep as any yet encountered.

A few oak trees grew close to the lip of the gorge, some of them on the very edge and slanting over the abyss as if straining to gaze down upon the mysteries below. Under one of these, as they walked around a point of chaparral, they came face to face with a big brown bear. He was an industrious bear and had not seen them nor smelled them, as the slight breeze that was astir was blowing in their faces. His majesty was sitting on his haunches, profile toward the surprised adventurers, with both paws to his mouth and with huge jaws working. As they came to a stop he lowered his body to all fours as lightly as a squirrel, for all his several hundred pounds of weight, picked up an acorn with one paw, and broke the shell of it with the butt of the other paw. He carried the kernel to his mouth and chonked with satisfaction. He sat erect again, saw the intruders, lowered both paws droopingly in abject surprise, and, with a startled *Wuff*, wheeled and went lumbering off at astonishing speed.

At the end of about fifteen shuffling leaps he swung abruptly toward the precipice and disappeared between an overhanging oak and an upstanding rock.

But for him, then, Charmian and Dr. Shonto would have walked directly past what seemed to be an animal-made trail that zigzagged down into the Valley of Arcana, the gateway of which was the monumentlike stone and the twisted black oak. They halted in the pass and heard the rattling of stones below and the scraping footsteps of the fleeing bear. A trail, narrow but plainly outlined, descended along the side of a portion of the precipice less steep than heretofore. The brush that grew over it here and there had been scraped of its bark in many places, and the smooth wood showing through had been polished by contact with the hair of various animals that had ascended and descended the trail for unreckoned years. The stones protruding from the earth were claw-scratched and eroded.

"I christen thee Bear Pass," saluted Charmian. "Can we go where that bear can, Doctor?"

"He may be bound for a den in the side of the precipice," suggested Shonto. "The trail may lead only to that. But it's worth a trial, provided—"

"Well?"

"It's narrow," finished the physician. "I wouldn't care to meet that bear down there, and find it necessary to argue the right of way with him with this .22."

"We won't argue," said Charmian. "It isn't polite. We'll excuse ourselves and go back. It's his trail, anyway. Let's try it. But I wish I hadn't crowed so loudly when I outcrawled you in the chaparral. I feel sick and dizzy every time I look over the edge. And on a narrow trail, with that chasm grinning up at me—*whew*! Don't you remember the iron rail at the edge of the great boulder overlooking the forest at El Trono de Tolerancia? I had to have it there. I never dared to stand and look without the feel of that iron pipe in my hands."

"Don't let that worry you," he cheered her. "Try to make it. Don't think of the chasm. Don't look at it. Keep your eyes on the trail. But if you get dizzy and nauseated let me know. I'll fix you up. Don't want to do it, though, unless it becomes necessary. But, being a doctor, I realize what a terrible sensation it is for one who suffers that way. It's dangerous, too. I never feel it myself. I would have made a wonderful mechanic at erecting the framework of skyscrapers."

He smiled at her encouragingly. "I'll go ahead," he said. "Keep close to me and think of something pleasant."

With a brave but wan little smile she fell in behind him, and he started along the descending shelf that followed the wall of the cavern.

It was dangerously narrow, a ticklish piece of business to follow it. Above them rose a craggy wall, growing in height as they progressed slowly downward. Occasionally the trail grew wider, but this usually occurred above a slope that was less precipitous. They wound in and out as the trail rounded gashes that extended from the lip above to the valley's floor.

"I'll tell you what," said Shonto, stopping suddenly and facing her: "This is not a natural trail, by any means. Though it's ages old, there are evidences left of the work of man. This shelf has been hacked in the cañon wall by somebody. It's preposterous to believe that animals—even wild goats or bighorn sheep—could have climbed up and down along this wall and eventually worn a level trail. They can go almost where a fly can, but they never could have struggled along this wall in its natural state."

"But who could have built it?" asked Charmian.

"I'm only too eager to find out," returned the doctor. "We may discover something mighty valuable down there on the floor. And I'm convinced that the trail extends entirely down. I've seen deer tracks. I don't believe deer would travel this trail, where there is not a blade for them to nibble, unless they were bound for the grass and the water down below. I've noticed 'coon tracks and skunk tracks and coyote tracks, too—but no sign of a man track. Yet men built this trail—hacked it in the side of this stone wall. I'll show you the next time I see a place where this is evident."

They went on, Charmian's face white, her upper teeth grasping her lower lip. She felt faint and vertiginous. Her knees shook. But she marched on bravely, hugging the upstanding wall on her left.

They came to a portion of the descent where the trail was little more than eighteen inches in width. Above them an absolutely perpendicular wall upreared itself. Below them yawned the abyss, at its very feet the green river, which swung in to the wall in a great bend from the meadows. To follow that eighteen-inch shelf would be like walking along the eaves trough of a house.

Charmian came to a halt. "Oh, I can't! I can't!" she moaned piteously. "I can't go on another step, Doctor! Don't ask me to! I'm—oh, I'm ill! I'm—I'm—"

His long arms closed about her, and she dropped her head on his breast, sobbing nervously, shaking like an aspen.

"There-there-there!" he soothed. "Don't worry. I'll fix you up. Lie down, now, and look up. That'll give you courage and relieve you. I'll fix you up so you can walk a tight rope and laugh."

He eased her to the ground and made her lie on her back. Her pretty face was dirty, and the tears had wriggled down her cheeks and washed elongated hieroglyphics in the grime. She gulped and licked her lips and looked up bravely into the heavens.

"There! There!" Shonto had removed his pack and was fumbling within for his medicine case. "Fix you up in a minute. Then you'll feel like climbing telegraph poles."

He was bending over her now. He took hold of one arm and pushed up the sleeve. She felt him squeezing the flesh. Then came a little stab of pain, and she rolled her eyes to see the glitter of a hypodermic syringe in his strong fingers.

"Wh-what did you do to me?"

"Hush! Never mind. Lie still a little and you'll feel dandy. Just a shot of cocaine. Feel it yet?"

"Ye-yes, I believe I do. I seem to be floating—floating; I'm getting light as a feather. My stars! I was never so happy in my life! I want to get up."

"Of course you do," chuckled Shonto. "Not only that, but you want to tell the world, when you get up, that you're equal to about anything, don't you?"

"Yes, I want to flap my wings and crow, even if I am a hen. I don't care for anything. I'm a whizgimp. Mary Temple says that a whizgimp is a person who is happy, even though he knows one more hot day will send him to the bug house."

She sat up suddenly and unexpectedly, turned to her knees, and in springing lightly to her feet with a glad little laugh, her foot struck the medicine case.

With a muttered oath the doctor sprawled in the trail and grasped at it. His frantic fingers touched it, but the contact served only to push it over the edge, and it went rattling and bounding down the cliff into the green waters of the river.

"Come on!" Charmian giggled. "Let it go! What's the difference! Lead out—I'm crazy to get down into the Valley of Arcana! And I can run along that narrow shelf and laugh while I'm about it!"

CHAPTER XVIII
IN THE PALM OF THE MOUNTAINS

SHONTO and his artificially elated companion continued their journey down the side of the steep cliffs without further mishap. The girl had taken the lead, stepping with a firm, springy stride, all horror of the abyss gone by reason of the potent drug. She was fearless but never reckless. The doctor had known that this would be the result of the hypodermic injection, so he did not worry about her safety and made no objection to her going first.

Nevertheless he was worried—worried as never before. A great calamity had come upon all that were concerned in the expedition, but only Dr. Shonto knew that this was true. The lost medicine case was responsible for it. It was so prodigiously serious that his homely face had turned a shade paler, and his mind was struggling desperately with the problem that it presented for him alone to solve.

Eventually the pair rounded the last switchback, and followed a gently sloping trail, quite wide, to the level floor of the valley. They came out upon the floor through a rocky pass, an eighth of a mile above the point where the green river swung in so abruptly to the foot of the cliffs. The land was wooded here. Sycamores, cottonwoods, water oaks, live oaks, willows and alders bespoke a more temperate clime than they had passed through since hours before they reached the cabin of Shirttail Henry Richkirk. The valley was lower than Ranger Reed had estimated, and the explorers had entered the Upper Sonoran Life Zone, where existence would be less problematical during rigorous seasons in the wilderness.

There was little underbrush. The grass, though frost-nipped, was still green. Digger pines were sprawling, their immense cones beneath the branches on the ground, many of them munched down to stems and scaly fragments by foraging squirrels. Linnets were singing in the willows. Wild canaries, mere dabs of pale yellow, flitted about importantly, bright-eyed, businesslike.

Charmian's brief sojourn in the land of Don't-give-a-whoop was over. The effects of the cocaine were waning. Her mouth was dry, and she was nervous and depressed. The reaction had set in, but the melancholy period would last little longer than the space of blissful unconcern for which it was the price.

The doctor took her hand. "You won't feel tough long," he consoled her, as, together, they invaded the solitary valley. "I would have given you a little touch of morphine to counteract the effects of the cocaine, but— Well, you know why I couldn't."

He heaved a sigh, and she looked up into his face questioningly.

"Does the loss of your medicine case mean so very much to you?" she asked.

"More than you know now," he said soberly. "Not only to me, but to you and Mary and Andy. But don't question me just now, please. My mind was never so busy before. I must decide what is best to do—and decide right. And every expedient that presents itself strikes me as impossible."

"Why, how serious you are! You worry me, Doctor. Won't you—"

"Not now," he interrupted hastily. "I shall be obliged to explain soon enough—after I have made my decision. To-morrow I'll tell you—well, tell you all that I dare tell."

He came to a halt as he finished speaking. They were following a well-defined trail that led them among natural obelisks of stone, tall and freakish. There was no other route to the floor proper of the valley. And at their very feet yawned a hole of large dimensions.

Shonto sank to his knees and looked in. "I thought as much," he muttered. "Look, Charmian! See those skeletons down in there?"

She knelt beside him, and when her eyes became accustomed to the gloom of the hole she saw the skeletons and skulls of many animals.

The walls of the hole were of solid rock, though masonry was not in evidence. The floor was level and many times wider than the mouth. This made the whole assume the shape of a funnel upside-down or an Indian wigwam.

"Why, they couldn't get out!" cried Charmian. "It is impossible to climb those walls."

"And you'll notice that the hole is directly in the middle of the narrow pass from the cliffs above," said he. "This, Charmian, is an Indian man-trap. In years gone by it was made here by residents of the valley to trap any enemies that might come down the trail to attack them. The hole was covered with light boughs, perhaps, with earth spread on top to hide them. I know this to be a trick of the Klamath Indians and the Pitt River tribes. But we are hundreds of miles from their stamping ground. We are in the rocks, you'll notice. There is not a grain of dirt near us. This accounts for the hole's not filling up with debris and disappearing through all these years. It's been gouged with infinite pains in comparatively solid stone. It's conclusive now that at one time the Valley of Arcana was inhabited and was the scene of tribal warfare. That was doubtless years before the fire swept down the forest and the chaparral locked the valley against intrusion."

"Oh, isn't it all interesting?" she cried, dark eyes aglow.

But the enthusiasm died out of them as she took note of the continued gravity of her companion's mien.

"Oh, you worry me so!" she complained again. "Please don't look so solemn. Tell me, and let me help."

"You can't," he told her, forcing one of those rare smiles that almost beautified his face. "I alone can work out an answer to the problem. And I will know the answer by to-morrow morning. Meantime I'll try my best to forget it."

A little farther on they found another man-trap, similar to the first. Then they left the cemeterial region of obelisks and passed out upon the broad floor of the cañon.

Here yellow California poppies were blooming late among the grasses, their orange-gold beauty staying the destructive hand of old Jack Frost as a soft answer turneth away wrath. The air was warm, delectable. The willows and cottonwoods were losing their leaves, but as yet their branches were far from nude. Over a carpet of grass the explorers wandered toward the river and the untarnished land about it—toward grotesque cliffs that in the distance upreared themselves from the level land, toward enchanted forests that intrigued them from afar.

Charmian's depression had gone. She was bright-eyed, vivacious, eager as a child. Shonto subdued his gloomy thoughts and made himself enter into the spirit of the quest; for he knew that, for him, there might not be another day in the valley that they had come so far to see.

They reached the river. It was wide and deep, and the jade-green hue of its waters that had lured them from above no longer was revealed. Height and distance had given the river colour, for now it was like any other clear, cold mountain stream. Its course was boulder-strewn, its bottom often pebbly. Large trout flashed in the sunlit riffles, where the water was like shaved ice, or lay like amber pencils in shaded pools.

They came upon ancient bridge abutments, fashioned of large stones, the crumbling red adobe mortar still to be seen in the crevices. Once a bridge had spanned the river at this point, probably merely a long pine log, axed to flatness on the upper side, and suspended between the pillars, Shonto said. They followed the river's course, almost despairing of finding a crossing. The doctor shot a jackrabbit sleeping under a bush, long ears laid back along his spine. They continued up the river for an hour, through a forest of oaks and alders and an occasional spruce; then they came to a narrow place through which a torrent roared. Here grew handily a clump of straight, tall alders, and with his hunting axe Shonto set about felling one so that it would fall across the cataract and bridge the gap for them.

Alders are not tough-fibred, and soon the tree was swaying. It leaned nearly in the right direction, and Charmian pushed at it as he completed the last few strokes. It groaned and started down. Shonto sprang up and aided the girl at pushing, then jerked her back to safety as the tree crashed down. It fell directly athwart the stream, with each end resting on solid stone.

Shonto crossed with both packs, walking sidewise, cautiously springing the trunk to test its strength. Then he returned to Charmian, face to the front, stepping easily and confidently.

"A romance is never complete," he smiled, "until the he character has carried the she character from one side of a stream of water to the other in his arms. Or maybe you'd prefer to go hippety-hop to the barber shop on my manly back."

She studied a moment. Then, with a trace of colour sweeping her face, she faltered:

"Which—whichever way you think better, Doctor."

He stooped and placed his long left arm behind her knees. His right arm he passed behind her back. He straightened, lifting her to his breast.

"Don't move," he cautioned, "and don't listen to the rush of the water. Relax. We're off!"

She closed both eyes as he stepped upon the trunk. Then she opened them again and looked up into his face. His strong jaw was set, she noted, but not a tremor did his body convey to hers. The roaring of the cataract was in her ears. Again she felt faint and dizzy. But without hesitation he placed one foot firmly and elastically before the other on the swaying bridge, until he stepped from it to the solid rocks on the other side.

"Nothing to it, was there?" he laughed, without a sign of nervousness, as he gently stood her on her feet.

"You have wonderful control over yourself, haven't you?" she said. "You never even trembled."

"Didn't I?" He was looking straight into her eyes. "I thought I was shaking like a leaf—especially when I reached this side and just before I set you down."

"Why, how funny! You certainly weren't frightened."

"No, tempted," said Shonto, while Charmian's face flushed crimson.

They wandered through an open forest of immense live and black oaks, with gnarled trunks and bulbous boles, and roots moss-upholstered where they were exposed. Gray moss hung from the upper limbs, draped and festooned with the delicacy of nature's artistry. Wild grape vines clambered in all directions, drooped in loops down the trunks of lofty trees, or extended in masses from the ground to the topmost branches like the standing rigging of a sailing ship. The clusters of grapes were ripe and ready to fall with their seed to the earth from whence they sprang.

They came upon large flat-topped stones, in which holes the size of a man's head had been gouged. In these the Indian squaws had powdered the acorns to make flour for their native bread, using heavy stone pestles as pulverizers.

A half-mile from the river they suddenly entered a clearing, studded with tall, monumental stones of granite, and with wide-branched oaks scattered about here and there. In the middle were the ruins of a house—the remnants of what had been a large house built of stones and sod and poles.

"That," said Shonto, "speaks plainly of some Northern tribe. The Northern Indians were further advanced than the tribes of Southern and Central California. The stone abutments back there made me believe that a tribe of comparatively high intelligence once occupied this valley. This ruin confirms it. Few of the California tribes built large public houses, as this undoubtedly was, for their ceremonial dances and big dinners and other social activities. I have never told you—for I hadn't the slightest idea that we'd find evidences of Indian life in the valley—but I've made quite a hobby of studying the aborigines of the Pacific Slope. So has Andy. We took it up together while nosing around in the mountains and on the desert, and we became intensely interested. I wish I could—" He came to a stop and gave her a look that was as near an admission of discomfiture as she had ever seen him reveal. "It's getting late. No doubt there's a spring close by, for this evidently is the site of the old village. Let's camp for the night and cook our rabbit."

Close by the ruins of the community house they located the spring. It was in a ferny dell with mossy banks. Charmian stooped for water and saw a white object a little distance off, half hidden by the drooping fronds. Instinctively she knew what it was. She rose and walked around to it. It was the tibia bone of a human being, and, scattered here and there throughout the ferns, she discovered the remainder of the skeleton, including the skull.

It gave her somewhat of a shock, but in the days to follow she was to grow accustomed to finding the bones and skulls of men in every conceivable place. This scatteration, the doctor held, bespoke the extinction of the tribe from the ravages of some epidemic—possibly smallpox—rather than a war of annihilation. Particularly so because no weapons were discovered near skeletons they found on open land.

The broiled jackrabbit was appetizing, for their stomachs were turned against salt meat and jerky. Though the air was frosty, the evening in the protected valley was pleasant, the smoke of the incense cedar of their campfire sweet. Dr. Inman Shonto had been taciturn during the preparations for supper and the coming night. His face was grave, his eyes thoughtful. Finally Charmian asked:

"Your case would sink, of course, wouldn't it?"

"I saw it sink out of sight," he replied. "There were some surgical instruments in it that made it heavy. And the river must be deep where it fell, with that sheer wall above it. Besides, all of my medical supplies that were not in corked bottles would be ruined, provided we could drag it up. It's a goner."

They made no further mention of the subject until the meal was over and Shonto, having heaped more wood on the coals, leaned back against the hole of a tree with pipe aglow.

He puffed thoughtfully for several minutes, while the girl gazed into the leaping flames, silent, sensing that her companion was nerving himself to lay his troubles before her. Finally he knocked the dottle from his pipe, pocketed it, and looked at her with a brotherly smile.

"I have decided sooner than I thought I should," he began. "So you may as well know the worst to-night. I don't think I'll have reached a better solution by morning."

He smiled again, patiently, as does a strong man in the face of threatening disaster.

"Charmian," he said, "to-morrow I must start back to Mary and Andy and leave you here alone. I'll get Andy and send him on to you, while I make an effort to take Mary back to Shirttail Henry's—or at least as far as Mosquito. Then I go on to civilization, while you and Andy wait for me to return to the Valley of Arcana. I'll probably come back to you in an aeroplane. Only by following that plan can Andy Jerome be saved."

CHAPTER XIX
RIDDLES

CHARMIAN was gazing across the fire at Shonto, half bewildered at his blunt statement. She had known that Andy was concerned in the disaster that had befallen the party, for long since she had connected the little tablets which he took daily with the loss of the medicine case.

"Has Andy told you anything of his physical troubles?" Shonto questioned.

"A little," she replied. "When we were at Jorny Springs with Leach and Morley. He told me about the period in his boyhood that he can't remember. He told me that it was necessary for him to take his tablets daily. Some kind of heart trouble, isn't it?"

The doctor nodded gravely. "Andy doesn't hesitate to tell about it," he said. "I imagined that you knew. Well—"

"Pardon me just a moment," she interrupted. "You haven't said outright that it is heart trouble, Doctor." "Have you any reason to think otherwise?"

"Yes—now. It seems to me that you are still reticent—virtually evasive. You aren't a practised dissimulator, Doctor. Why do you try it?"

"I'll be frank with you," he said, "if you'll be as frank with me. Will you?"

"Of course."

"I shall have to ask for your display of frankness first," he went on. "You must answer this question before I shall feel at liberty to tell you why I have been close-mouthed: In the big cañon that night before you and I left, did Andy ask you to marry him?"

Her face went red, but she shook her head.

"I believe you," he said. "But Andy would be too excited to think of asking you to marry him, perhaps. He—both of you—would take marriage for granted. So I must ask another question: Didn't he tell you that he loves you, and didn't you surrender yourself to him?"

Her long lashes covered her dark eyes, and for a space she declined to answer. Then she lifted her head and looked him straight in the face.

"I suppose," she said slowly, "that, according to the standardized procedure, I ought to say, 'What right have you to ask me that?' But you have the right— I suppose. Anyway, I consider it a fair question, and I'll answer it as fairly. He did, and I did. But—but how did you know, Doctor?"

The doctor's laugh was brief and bitter. "When you two returned to camp," he informed her, "the announcement couldn't have been plainer if you had pinned placards on your breasts. I knew what had happened. So did Mary Temple."

"Well?"—almost defiantly.

"Well, I suppose there's nothing to be said. Theoretically I should back gracefully away, murmuring my congratulations. But I'll not do that. I don't give up so easily, Charmian. I am convinced that you and I are mated, and that you and Andy are not. I think that it would be a great misfortune for both of us if we don't become man and wife. But I'll play the game fair and square—with both you and Andy. And this desire to play square is what has kept my mouth closed on so many occasions. I won't tell you why I think it unwise for you to marry Andy Jerome. On the contrary, I'll go out and leave you two here together and make every effort to get back with more medicine before you can learn for yourself that I am the man you should have for a husband instead of him. It's hard, Charmian—hard to play square, when I hold my rival's future in the hollow of my hand. But the ethics of my profession demand that I do all in my power to save him, and my conscience demands the same.

"So to-morrow I must leave you, hoping that I can get back in time. There is no other way. I'll make it back to Mary and Andy, and send Andy on here. With the aid of a compass and the directions that I can give him he will never miss the pass into the valley. You must hoist a garment or a blanket on a pole, which he will be able to see from the top of the wall and all the way down. Or a smudge of damp leaves will send up a stream of smoke to direct him to you.

"Andy is a master mountaineer and woodsman. It is born in him; he inherited it from his Alps-climbing ancestors. He will be able to supply you with food while you are waiting for me to return. But listen carefully: As soon as he comes, have him show you how to make rabbit snares and pitfalls and deadfalls, so that you will be able to get game if he becomes unable to do it for you. You two get to work at once gathering all the nuts and acorns you can—and you'd better be working at it before he comes. Stow them away. Have Andy show you how to pulverize the acorns and make Indian bread of the flour. Gather huckleberries—all you can—I saw a patch of them up the river from where we crossed to-day. The berries will be ripe now. Then you'll find nuts in the cones of the piñon pines. Andy has a little fishing tackle. There should be mountain trout in the river. If Indians could subsist in this valley without drawing upon civilization for supplies, trust Andy to do it. But the important point is that you must make him teach you all that he knows about foraging in the wilderness before he—before he becomes unable to help you. For that may happen."

"You are not making yourself clear, Doctor," Charmian told him. "Why is all this necessary? Why can't we all go out together? In other words, if Andy can get here to me why can't he make it out to Shirttail Henry's or Mosquito? And why can't Mary Temple come here with Andy, if she is able to go with you over the mountains?"

"Mary deceived you, with my knowledge," confessed Shonto. "Her ankle isn't sprained. She has a broken rib. She could never crawl through that chaparral. It would break her in two, almost. But she can walk in an erect position, after a fashion, with me to help her. Anyway, there's nothing else to be done; we'll have to try it. And Andy—"

"Why did Mary Temple tell me she had a sprained ankle when she had broken her rib?" demanded Charmian.

"She wanted to force you and me into the wilderness together," explained Shonto, without a sign of contrition. "That's what I believe now. I know she doesn't approve of Andy Jerome as a husband for you. And she has hinted that she wants you to marry me. That's frank enough, isn't it? But she told me that she was afraid of putting a stop to your expedition if she confessed to a broken rib. She knew that she could walk with her rib broken—see?—and thought that you would insist on taking her back and spoiling the fun. But if she pleaded a sprained ankle, you would imagine that she couldn't walk one way or the other, and it would be just as well to leave her there until she could walk again, while you went on with your hunt for the valley. It worked out to her satisfaction, as you see."

"And now you think she deliberately planned to get you and me to continue the trip together?"

"I'm afraid so," smiled Shonto, "though I give my word it didn't occur to me at the time. I never gave a thought to the old trick of making one person think he has had a square deal in drawing straws by the use of two whole matches. You see, there was no short match for Andy to draw. Both matches were whole. The one who drew the long straw was elected to stay in the cañon. When Andy saw that he had drawn an entire match, he didn't think to ask to see the other one, but considered himself defeated then and there."

"I think it was abominable of Mary Temple!" the girl said sharply.

"Perhaps it was so," admitted Shonto. "Nevertheless, the fact remains that she was, and always is, working for what she thinks your best interests. And it struck me as almost noble of her to feign a sprained ankle in order to keep you on the quest. Sending me out with you occurred to her later, I think. At the time she played only to keep your expedition moving—and it called for a certain amount of sacrifice for a crippled, middle-aged woman to remain in that deep cañon all alone."

Charmian made no further comment on Mary's well-meant perfidy. She thought deeply for a long time, and when she spoke she reverted to a question that still remained unanswered:

"Why can't Andy go out with the rest of us if he is able to get to the Valley of Arcana?"

"It will require a great deal more time for us to get out with the crippled Mary than it will for Andy to find you here," Shonto explained. "And he might— It might happen that he would succumb on the way. Andy Jerome, Charmian, is an experiment. I know that he can hold out for three or four days, but how much longer I don't know, because I've never experimented with him to the extent of shutting off his medicine to find out. Andy is my friend—his family have been my friends for many years. So I really don't know what would happen if we were many days on the back trail or if a blizzard came on and left us storm-bound in the mountains. But here in the Valley of Arcana, where everything is smiling and there will be an abundance of food for some time to come, he will be safe with you to care for him. I simply can't risk taking him out."

"It's the loss of his supply of tablets, of course," murmured the widow. "Why didn't you leave him a sufficient supply?"

"He has as much as he ever carries when I am with him," said the doctor. "I usually carry the main stock when we are out in the wilderness together. I have always thought it safer to keep the greater part of it myself. I don't go into so many difficult places as Andy does. I don't take the risks that he does. Then if something happened to his supply, I'd still have enough for him. Perhaps it was foolish for me to bring along any at all on the trip from the cañon, but I have become so accustomed to keeping it in my medicine case that I followed the usual procedure. I knew that Andy would not be content to stay with Mary all the time. He'll be scouring the hills and cañons in search of things to interest him. And he always takes his tablets. If he had all of them, he might lose them, as I did. You see, that's the way I reasoned. I'm Andy's guardian—a poor one, I confess now. And the difficulty is that I'm never free to talk over his malady with him or others. To be a little more frank still, it is a secret, even to Andy himself. This time I reasoned wrong— if I reasoned at all—and simply didn't do as I did from force of habit. And Andy must have more medicine just as soon as I can get it to him, for I don't know how long he'll last without it when his present supply is gone.

"So there's the nut-shell truth of the situation. Mary can't come here; Andy doesn't dare to try to make it out. You must stay here in the valley and take care of Andy. I must get Mary out and hurry to a point where I can send a wire for more tablets. There's no other alternative. I've thought it all out; looked at the matter from every angle."

"But—but what shall I do?" she puzzled. "What can I do to help Andy? What am I to expect?"

"You can do nothing," replied the doctor. "I mean, I can't give you any instructions. Neither can Andy. When—if anything happens, you will soon know what to do. I really can't tell you any more, Charmian. It wouldn't be fair to him. For it may transpire that nothing at all will happen—and that's what I'm hoping for. I must trust to Fate, for I myself am ignorant of what will be the result if Andy's supply of tablets runs out before I can get back with more. Neither do I know how soon the result will begin to show. And, as I said, in fairness to him I must not prepare you for anything simply because nothing at all may happen. For more reasons than one I don't want you to marry Andy Jerome; but I'll not be the one to tell you anything that might keep you from doing so."

"Why, Doctor!" she cried. "You've done nothing but bewilder me. I can't imagine what you're talking about at all. It's all riddles."

"I realize that," he confessed, "but I consider myself helpless to make the thing clearer."

"I don't believe Andy has heart trouble at all!" she said half angrily. "It's something about the glands, I know. That accounts for your repeated refusals to tell me much about your work. Isn't that right?"

He nodded in agreement.

Another period of staring into the flames on her part; then she cried passionately:

"Oh, I don't want to stay here alone and wait for Andy! And I'm afraid—afraid of what may happen to him! But if I must stay, it's cruel of you to leave me in ignorance of what to expect. And I can't even talk it over with Andy, it seems."

"No, he knows less about it than you do," Shonto told her. "His parents and I have deceived him into thinking he has had heart trouble for years. And no one but his parents and I know the truth."

"Oh, that sounds terrible! You think I shouldn't marry Andy, and yet—"

"If Andy remains all right," he cut in quickly, "there is no positive reason why you shouldn't marry him. I think, however, that he is not the man for you—and it's fair enough for me to make that statement for the simple reason that I'm convinced *I'm* the man for you. I refuse to call to your mind any of Andy's faults. I have enough of my own. If he has any, you must find them out for yourself. But I'll make you marry me instead of him because you will see that I'm the man to make your life complete, and that you're the woman to make mine complete. You don't love Andy. I know you don't. You merely think you do. His magnificent young manhood has carried you off your feet, and you've not gone deeper into the matter. Blind, physical love you have given him—but it will pass, Charmian. And that's enough—positively all. We'll turn in and try to forget it all for to-night. And to-morrow early I'm off to send Andy to you. I know you'll care for him if—if he needs it. But if you believe in God, pray to him that he won't! Good night. My bed is over there by the big oak. Call me if you need me for anything."

CHAPTER XX
THE INTERIM OF DOUBTS

CHARMIAN did not begin sobbing until, standing at the edge of the grove that surrounded the ruins of the ancient village, she saw a tiny speck moving slowly up the narrow trail which zigzagged along the sides of the cliffs from the Valley of Arcana. The moving speck was Dr. Shonto, and he was leaving her alone in a vast wilderness, filled with doubts and dread and loneliness and grave forebodings. She sank to the ground, laid her arms on a fallen tree, and drenched them with her tears.

He had held her hand a long time in parting, smiling at her in his patient, benign way. His smile had been encouraging, though he had not told her to be brave. It was a compliment to her courage, she thought, that he had taken it for granted that she would be intrepid and had considered mere words of emboldenment as idle. He realized, she reasoned, that a girl who would set out to accomplish such an enormous task as hunting for an unexplored valley in an unmapped wilderness would have the bravery to meet with cheerfulness any unforeseen emergency that might arise.

When her cry was over she returned to camp and began to work as the surest way of overcoming her loneliness. Not many provisions were left, as Shonto had been obliged to take something along with him to sustain life between the valley and the waiting pair in the cañon. Charmian searched for and found a huckleberry patch, black with fruit which so far had resisted frost. She spent the remainder of the morning gathering berries, but realized as she worked that, since she had no way of preserving them, they represented food only for temporary use. She was not fond of fruit, either, but she forced herself to eat quantities of the juicy huckleberries at noon in order to save the staples in her pack.

That afternoon, wandering through the grove, she came upon a hut which was fairly well preserved. The construction was typically Indian. Ordinarily such huts are made by first sinking in the ground a hole about five feet in depth. Around this pit stout poles are planted deep. These are bent in at the tops until they nearly touch, and are bound about with bark or strips of hide. The hole at the top allows the smoke to go through, and it also serves as an entrance. A short ladder or notched pole on the inside leads to the hole, and leaning against the structure on the outside is a corresponding pole or ladder. The entire framework of poles is covered with earth to a depth of several inches.

In this instance, however, the pit was a natural one, formed in solid rock. It probably had been a pothole in an ancient creek-bed. With this substantial beginning, the builder of the hut had constructed the above-ground portion along sturdier lines. Instead of poles he had used the trunks of small redwood trees ten inches in diameter, and no other soft wood resists the ravages of time so well. Unable to sink the butts in the solid stone, he had dragged great slabs of rock and piled them about the base of his dwelling as anchors and had covered the whole with earth in far greater quantities than are commonly employed.

The result was that he had left a monument to his diligence and sound constructive principles, and it gave promise of a sheltered home for Charmian.

She noted most of the details when she had found an ancient notched pole and used it as a ladder to climb to the entrance in the roof. Shonto had explained the construction of these huts to her, so she knew how to go about getting into the seemingly doorless hovel. There was not much earth left on the sloping sides, but the straight, peeled redwood logs were close together, and the cracks between were narrow ones.

The light filtering in between these cracks revealed the interior as she clung to the top of the crude ladder and looked down through the hole.

As she had shudderingly expected, the first things that she saw were human skeletons, yellow rather than bleached, on the stone floor below her. The notched pole of the interior had broken off at the middle, and the two parts, old and decayed, lay prone. She dreaded to enter, but she thought that she must find a better refuge than the broad, unprotected outdoors. There probably were mountain lions in the valley, and maybe grizzlies were not altogether extinct in this remote region. She sat astride the upper ends of the logs and contrived to drag her notched pole up the side and lower it through the hole. To live in there she must remove the skeletons, and she dreaded to touch them as she had never before dreaded anything in her life.

She clambered down to the rock bench surrounding the hole. She crawled over the edge and lowered herself backward into the five-foot pit. There were three skeletons, the bones of which were unscattered. Dry, brown skin clung to them, wrinkled and harder than a drum-head. Mats of black hair had slipped from the skulls and made cushions under them. With a feeling of deep repugnance she set about her inevitable task and began lifting the dry bones to the bench above. Many of them she later was able to pitch through the hole in the roof, to hear them clattering down the redwood logs to the ground outside. Larger portions that persisted in hanging together she laboriously carried to the top and dropped.

When this disagreeable task had been finished she gave more attention to the interior.

Dirt had sifted in, of course, and the stone floor was partially covered with it. Rain also would enter at every crack and settle in a pool in the rocky pit. She wondered if, when the hut was in shape, the earth thrown over it had kept it dry. If it were to snow before it rained, she thought, the snow covering might be effective in that respect. She knew that Eskimos lived in huts of snow, but she did not know what held them up.

She found red pottery, crude and interesting—water *ollas* and great bowls and smaller dishes. She found a skin garment, well tanned and well preserved. It had been inlaid with brilliant duck scalps, the greater part of which had succumbed to the erosive hand of time. She found nose rings and goose-quill ornaments and arrowheads of flint and obsidian and a bowl-shaped basketwork cap which once had been adorned with the bright feathers of woodpeckers and jays, for the remnants of them lay all about it. There were elk-horn knives and hatchets and awls of the sharpened bones of mule deer. And on a slab of bone, taken from the skeleton of some large animal and cut square, she found a crude carving unmistakably depicting the rather revolting episode of a woman vomiting up a frog.

She forgot her troubles, digging in the dirt for more relics with the primitive tools of the dead. She found a fish spear with a yew-wood shaft and a head of volcanic glass—a veritable treasure. She did not notice the darkening of the hut as the ephemeral winter sun sank swiftly nearer to the saw-tooth cliffs that towered about the Valley of Arcana. Then of a sudden almost no light at all streamed in through the cracks, and the hut was dark and cold. She shuddered, scrambled to the bench, climbed the notched pole as hurriedly as possible, and, not stopping to drag it out after her, slid down the sloping side and landed in a heap on the ground.

Twilight had come. Night would follow soon, with the tall cliffs to shut off the last remnants of the sunlight from the valley. She hurried to her camp, spread her blankets, and pondered over what she would eat for supper.

There was not much choice. She had a little bacon, a little flour, a little coffee, a quantity of salt, and a can of baking powder. Her huckleberries were heaped upon the ground, and she looked at them askance. She had dined on huckleberries at noon—had forced herself to do so. She decided to fry some bacon for the resulting grease, to be used in making biscuits. The bacon she would not eat then, but would have it cold for supper to-morrow evening. One meal a day of staples was all that she could afford, she told herself, until Andy came with more supplies. If he came!

She strove to keep Andy from her thoughts. To think of him was to worry— and she must not worry. Time for that when he came to her—when they could worry together and he could comfort her. She was going to fight her way bravely through the ordeal until he came—and then she would relax and let him take the initiative and relieve her of the strain. But how long could he hold out? And what dread thing was threatening him? But there! She must not think of that. Dr. Shonto had consoled her with the repeated remark that perhaps nothing would happen at all, provided he—Shonto—was able to get back soon enough. Provided! But she shook her head resolutely and went to work at getting supper while the shadows of night enshrouded the valley and coyotes began their evening concert in the hills.

The days and nights that passed until the coming of the expected one were fraught with torture. Charmian was not afraid in the general meaning of the word, but the mysterious sink, so serene and quiet and remote, awed her and filled her with strange forebodings that she could not shuffle off. She spent the days at gathering acorns, scolded at frequently by Douglas squirrels who claimed the entire crop between the valley walls. The piñon nuts, too, they considered theirs, and told her so with angry chatterings, made more emphatic by the gestures of their jerking tails. A slight midnight rain brought to life near the river a bed of mushrooms of a variety which she had often gathered on the Marin hills across the bay from San Francisco. These she garnered eagerly, and they grew in quantities. She feasted on fresh ones for several meals, dipping them in thin batter and frying them in bacon grease, or stewing them. Many she dried. And then she bethought herself to dry wild grapes and huckleberries, whereupon a new and engrossing task took form. All day long she managed to keep busy. This helped to keep away the blues, and at night she found herself so weary that sleep came easily.

She had lighted her signal fire, heaping on green boughs to make dense smoke. There was little wind in the valley, and the smoke streamed aloft in a graceful spiral above the treetops. Every morning she rebuilt the fire and heaped on boughs when it was burning brightly. And now came a day when she stood often at the edge of the grove and scanned the zigzag trail into the sink with her binoculars. Or, gathering nuts and acorns and mushrooms in the open, stopped her work and trained her glasses about every fifteen minutes.

And at noon one day she was rewarded by the sight of a tiny speck descending along the trail. She shouted in her eagerness and loneliness, unmindful that her lover was miles away. She glanced once to make sure that the smoke was still streaming aloft from her signal fire, then began running toward the river. If she could bring herself to cross the log bridge she could run into the open on the other side and travel a long way in the direction of the northern cliffs before Andy had reached the bottom of the sink. She hesitated only a little when she reached the fallen tree, then climbed astride it and worked her way over the boiling water, gripping with hands and calves.

They sighted each other in one of the level meadows of the river bottom. Andy shouted to her; she shrilled a glad reply. Then both started running, came together panting for breath, and hung in each other's arms.

Then once more Charmian Reemy sobbed, this time with her tousled head on the broad shoulder of the man who loved her. She had promised herself this weeping spell as a reward for holding back her tears throughout the days and nights just past; and now she rewarded herself abundantly and without reserve. But hers were tears of gladness and relief. Nothing was to happen to Andy! The doctor had needlessly distressed her. Here he was in her arms, big and strong and virile and handsome as a god—what ever could happen to such a man! There was food in the valley—nuts and game and fish. And if the huckleberries would only last she would be content to live on them alone, while Andy was with her in the valley. The doctor might never return if he chose to leave them there together. What mattered it, when she had Andy? The Valley of Arcana had lost its grimness. It was a valley of happy smiles, blessed by nature, sun kissed, gloriously resplendent from wall to wall. It was warm noontide and the sun was overhead—and she was crying happily on Andy's shoulder.

"And had Mary Temple and the doctor started out when you left?" she asked finally, wiping her tears on a sleeve of her flannel shirt.

"Yes, dear—we all started at the same time. Doctor Shonto told me about Mary's faking a sprained ankle. She'll have a time of it with that broken rib, I'm thinking. But I guess there was no other way. What did the doctor tell you about me, Charmian?"

"He wouldn't explain anything," she answered. "Wouldn't warn me at all beyond telling me that I couldn't be of any help to you if—if anything happened."

"Don't worry," he told her lightly. "Nothing at all is going to happen. I have almost twice as much dope as Doctor Shonto thought I had; but still the quantity is small compared with the store he carried. Anyway, he wouldn't trust me to try and make the trip out on it, for some one would have had to return here for you, and days would have been wasted. But he cheered me up—and told me to pass it on to you—by saying that there probably was no danger at all, and that everything depended on his getting back to us in a couple of weeks or more. That ought to be easy for him."

"But if it snows heavily, Andy?"

"Not a sign of a cloud now. A little rain a couple of nights ago, but just a shower. Doesn't mean anything at all as regards the setting in of winter. In the altitudes it may snow, even, in June, July, and August—any time. He'll make it all right, and we'll all get out before snow flies.

"It all seems ridiculous to me, Charmian. Here I am as strong as an ox, healthy and whole, and enjoying life immensely. But I have been told ever since I can remember that if I don't take those infernal tablets regularly I'll die. Yet Doctor Shonto never has warned me against putting great strains on my heart. Always has struck me as a funny sort of heart trouble that I'm afflicted with. But I don't know anything about diseases of the heart. This can't be a common one, though, can it?"

"It's not your heart at all, Andy," she said. "The doctor told me so. It's something else—a secret between him and your parents. And I don't know what to expect if the doctor fails to get in before your tablets give out."

This continually worried her. The doctor had said that Andy's life depended on regular doses of the medicine, but he had not exactly warned her of death. There was something dreadful back of his solemn words which convinced her that Andy's state would be worse than death—a living death of some sort, her reason kept on torturing her.

"Well, no use to worry, sweetheart," he said lightly. "Chances are all of your fears are useless. Have you had plenty to eat? I brought every pound I could lug. There was plenty left for the doctor and Mary to get back to the cache on. They can load up fresh there. That is, Doctor Shonto can—Mary can't pack a pound. What have you been doing? Discovered anything? Doctor Shonto told me about his advising you to gather all the nuts and acorns you could before I came. Got any?"

"Yes—piles. I gathered them in order to forget myself."

"Good idea. Let's get to your camp now. I'm a wizard in the woods, and the doctor told me that the valley is well supplied with things to eat. I'll show you how to roast the pine nuts and make *bellota*—Indian acorn bread—and make traps and things. This will be a regular picnic for us, Charmian. Prettiest spot I ever saw. I'm keen to get to nosing around. We'll have the time of our young lives."

"Yes, everything will be interesting—now," said Charmian, with a happy sigh of relief. "If—if only—"

"There! There!" laughed Andy. "No 'if onlys' about it. Forget it and let's begin our castaway life with nothing but anticipation."

CHAPTER XXI
THE CAVE OF HYPOCRITICAL FROGS

THEY lived in an enchanted land, bright and tranquil under an Indian-summer sun while mid-day hours endured, crisp with frost of mornings, calmly cold throughout the nights.

Charmian had not transferred her dwelling-place to the redwood hut after all her labours at removing the ghastly reminders of a vanished clan. Andy, when he saw it, opined that it would be far from water-tight despite his efforts with a wooden shovel that he had made with hunter's axe and jackknife. What they wanted to do, he said, was to find a cave in the cliffs somewhere up the river. Who ever heard of castaways living in anything but a cave! And there must be caves in those craggy cliffs. Where was the romance of the Valley of Arcana if it could boast no caves? Anyway, he was not content to remain in the grove that harboured the ruined village. There were over a hundred square miles in the enchanted valley, and few of them had been explored.

They set off early the following morning, Charmian loaded with the packs, Andy carrying her store of nuts, acorns and half-dried fruit and mushrooms in a blanket. They struck out for the river, deciding to explore its mysteries first. If it was in reality the lost river of the upper benches, Andy wanted to see how it found its erratic way into the valley.

They crossed smiling meadows, lush with bronze-green grass. Once, from a little rise, they caught a glimpse of the distant blue lake. They came upon herds of deer which were too curious to continue their flight after the first startled dash, but turned and surveyed them in blank amaze. A skunk was hunting bugs in the grass, rooting in the turf, his plume asway above his striped back. The banks of the river were endowed with graceful willows, alders, yews, incense cedars, cottonwoods, oaks, California buckeyes, red madrones, spicy bays, and occasional pines and spruces, with grape vines crawling and climbing everywhere. The river bottoms were rank with huckleberry bushes, and Andy said:

"Find a bee tree and we'll get some honey and preserve those berries and grapes in Indian jars—if we find any more. Stretch a piece of hide over the mouth and seal it with spruce gum. Stay here all our lives, by golly! No? Yes?"

It was like a park, this Valley of Arcana. Meadows merged into woodland stretches or necks of timber, to continue on the other side as grassy and level as before. The river plunged over outcroppings of bedrock, often in foaming cataracts from ten to fifty feet in height. In a neck of woods, in a drift that had collected about the roots of trees, they found a large canoe. Flat bottomed it was, blunt at either end, and burned and gouged from solid sycamore. Near it on the river bank they found an ancient *temescal*, or Indian sweat house.

These were the men's clubs of the Rogue River Indians or the Klamaths, Andy said. The canoe, also, pointed either to these tribes or Pitt River tribes, all belonging to the north. The *temescals* were never entered by the women, he explained. The males lolled in them after bathing in the icy water, which usually followed a terrific sweat over heated stones, or beside a blazing fire. The canoe, he thought, might prove serviceable if they could discover some means of calking the checks and cracks that time had wrought in its sides and bottom.

They camped at noon by the river, and Andy cast a line for trout. They rose to the bait readily, some big ones so eager as to leap entirely from the water at the cast. They roasted them wrapped in leaves, and buried in the heated ground, Indian fashion. The trees were alive with grey squirrels, impish little Douglas squirrels, and impertinent chipmunks. Birds sang ceaselessly. Their tramp of the afternoon showed them herd after herd of deer, and once a herd of antelope. Quail, grouse, jackrabbits and the little "blue peter" rabbit in the plateau chaparral, ducks, mudhens and dabchicks on the river, a condor, rarest of California vultures, riding overhead in the beryl heavens. Closely flying flocks of wild pigeons threw hovering shadows across the valley, into which they swooped to feed on the bitter black berries of the cascara bush. As they neared a pyramidal mountain in the centre of the valley they saw bighorn sheep browsing off the brush.

Abreast the mountain they came upon rugged country, where the river plunged down incessantly in a hundred falls and cataracts. And here, as they crossed the ridge, Andy found his cave and made lengthy apology to the Valley of Arcana for doubting its claims to romance.

It was in the ridge of rocks that extended at right angles to the river on both sides. If they made a habitation of the cave there would be constantly in their ears the roar of the waterfall that found its way through the ridge and plunged down about thirty feet to the lower level. Centuries of the rushing water had worn down the ridge, and the stream leaped through a narrows, with the piled-up boulders towering above it on either side. On the side where the cave was located grew a clump of sucker redwoods, which had sprung up from a mother stump about six feet in diameter. Examination of the perdurable stump showed that the original tree had been felled with axes. Many years had elapsed since its fall, for the redwood is of tremendously slow growth, and the tall, slim suckers that surrounded the stump were a foot in diameter. Andy decided that he could cut down two of them and cause them to fall side by side directly across the chasm. This would give them a bridge from one rocky eminence to the other, and it would hang twenty feet or more above the waterfall.

Though all evidences of a beaten trail to the cave had disappeared, it was an easy matter to trace the upward progress of the one that had existed in the days of the lost tribe. Boulders of large size evidently had been rolled away from the most logical route. They wound their way in and out among the towering rocks to the mouth of the cave, probably seventy feet above the narrows. From below they had seen its gaping mouth, but were fearful that it would prove a shallow disappointment—a mere niche in the rocky hillside. But it turned out to be a substantial, denlike tunnel, forty feet or more in length.

Men had not fashioned it, but within they had moved huge boulders to one side or the other to make more room in the middle. Irregular stones had covered the floor, too, and smaller ones had been thrown into the crevices, with dirt piled on top, to level it off. The width and height were probably fifteen feet.

They found more skeletons, more pottery, more implements of war and the chase, and crude tools of stone and bone. The boulders inside were decorated, designs and hieroglyphics having been hacked below the surface. Some sort of red paint of a decidedly perdurable quality had been worked into the gouged lines. Once again Charmian saw an unhappy lady ridding herself of the frog that she had swallowed. But in this instance she did not suffer alone. If misery loves company, she must have been in an amiable mood, despite her throes. For no less than a dozen of her unfortunate sisters were engaged in a like performance on boulders and stony walls.

"I've got it, Charmian," Andy cried with the enthusiasm of an amateur ethnographer. "I know now what it means. The northern tribes had woman doctors, and they treated their patients by sucking the flesh. They were supposed to suck out the evil spirit that was tormenting them, and this evil spirit often took the form of a snake or a lizard or a frog. In order to make good, a doctress is said to have sometimes swallowed a live frog before beginning treatment; and when she threw it up the patient and his relatives were convinced that the faker had done her best. This was probably the cave of the doctresses. Say—doesn't it stand to reason?"

"How pleasant!" laughed Charmian. "I see now how the nursery term 'quack frog' had its birth. Let's remove the wizards' remains and take possession of the cave. Can we ever make it cheerful after what you've told me? I christen it the Cave of Hypocritical Frogs. That's rather long and confusing, but so the Indians might have called it had there been unbelievers. We could live in this cave indefinitely, Andy. It will be dry and warm, don't you think? I hope no bear has decided to hibernate here throughout the winter."

Somehow or other both of them were always unconsciously planning for a long stay in the Valley of Arcana. Andy had proposed hunting up a bee tree, the honey from which might be used in preserving grapes and huckleberries. He had planned a bridge over the waterfall, when a mile below they had passed a riffle which offered an easy fording. Now Charmian was looking at the cave in the light of a more or less permanent habitation. She thought of this directly after she had spoken and bit her lip in vexation. Wasn't Dr. Shonto to hurry right back to them? Two weeks, at the most, and he should be worming his way into the valley, searching the distances for the smoke of their signal fire. She threw off her sudden depression. It was best to be prepared. The fact that they were planning for months to come meant nothing. That was only the part of wisdom. And they had nothing else to do. What if they did leave behind them two weeks hence the results of their trifling labours in the valley? It was only play. Weren't they like children playing at the game of keeping house?

Andy removed the skeletons, cleaned house, carried their belongings up to the cave, and arranged things for their temporary comfort. Then he went to catch some trout in the swirling pool below the waterfall for the evening meal.

Charmian slept in the cave that night, Andy in the open. They were about and had breakfast early in the morning, and they spent the greater part of the day in carrying flat stones into the cave to be used in building a partition. The inner room was to be the girl's, while Andy would occupy the space within the mouth of the cave and guard her. They doubted whether there was anything to guard her from, but it seemed the proper thing to do.

When the stone partition was up Andy hacked at two of the redwood suckers with his hunter's axe until they fell almost side by side across the water. The top of the last to fall, however, was pitched off when it struck the top of the first down. This left a rather wide gap between the trunks, so they busied themselves at cutting and carrying poles, which they laid close together and parallel with the stream, from trunk to trunk.

"That'll make a better bridge than ever," Andy approved. "You won't be afraid to cross now. What next? Let's see—there's no particular hurry about sweating the bitterness out of the acorns, or furnishing our home, or anything like that. We can do all such things after the winter sets in." (There it was again!) "What d'ye say we go back and drag that canoe out of the drift pile and see what we can do toward filling the cracks?"

They spent a day at this task. Spruce gum, they found, filled the gaps admirably and stuck there, hardening when the clumsy craft was in the water. Andy got in it and guided it about with a makeshift paddle. But the current was swift and threatened to carry him down to one of the many cataracts, so he quickly beached the canoe and dragged it up on the pebbles until he had time to make a paddle that would serve.

They busied themselves during following days at turning the acorns from cold water into hot water, and reversing the process time and again to "sweat" out the bitterness. There were large stone mortars in the cave, and in these, with the pestles they found, they powdered nuts for their daily use and made rather tasteless bread and pasty *bellota* of the powder. Their grapes and huckleberries and mushrooms were thoroughly cured by now, and they stowed them away. They gathered acorns, loose piñon nuts, and buckeyes by the thousand, catching them like squirrels. The cones of the piñon pines they heaped in piles and built fires over them, which loosened the nuts and roasted them at one operation. Andy taught Charmian to make and set figure-four traps for rabbits. Of willow boughs they made traps for quail, and gathered the larger grass seeds for bait. They were constantly employed, and ten days slipped by before they were aware. Now and then clouds glided across the blue dome above, but the weather remained dry and tranquil, though noticeably colder. Daily Andy trapped game for food, for it was an easy matter to lure the quail and rabbits and grouse. They jerked rabbits over cedar-wood fires and hung them in the cave. Charmian had set her foot down on shooting deer, though Andy had a heavy-calibre rifle. They were so tame and inquisitive and confident, with their big glistening eyes fixed upon the usurpers in friendly wonder, that to kill one of them seemed to her wantonly cruel. She turned her back when Andy took live quail and grouse from the traps and dispatched them. The rabbits, caught in deadfalls, died instantly under falling stones or logs.

And so the short days passed until the sky was overcast with mackerel clouds and the wind rustled the dead leaves of the deciduous trees and sent them scurrying through the air. Andy's hair was growing long. They had missed a day or two, they thought, but they knew that Dr. Shonto should be nearing the valley on his return. All day long they kept their signal fire smouldering near the mouth of the Cave of Hypocritical Frogs, and from it a thin stream of smoke rose constantly.

Then one morning Andy confessed to Charmian that his stock of tablets was growing alarmingly low, and that for the past four days he had been splitting them and taking only half doses.

That night the air over the valley was filled with a peculiar moan. All seemed quiet about them on the valley's floor, but up above the moan continued, a weird, dismal battle anthem of the mountain winds. Next morning soft snowflakes were falling into the sink, while up above a great storm raged, and snow-dust blew from the tops of distant peaks in awe-inspiring banners half a mile in length. The war banners of the mountain winds, mobilizing for the grand charge and chanting triumphantly!

CHAPTER XXII
DR. SHONTO RIDES ALONE

DOWN on the desert, a day's journey in the saddle from Diamond H Ranch, where the pilgrims to the Valley of Arcana had left their cars, lived an old man named Gustav Tanburt. His rancho had its existence because of an oasis similar to the one at Diamond H, and he had prospered throughout the years that he had lived there as a desert rat.

Through his broad acres passed a road extending at right angles to the road that entered the property of his distant neighbour. This last-mentioned road—the one by which Charmian's party had reached Diamond H Ranch—went no farther, and the trackless sweeps of the desert separated the two properties. But Tanburt's road was moderately well travelled. Freighters driving eight- and ten- and twelve-horse teams pursued it on their way to a distant mining community in the mountains. Gus Tanburt's ranch was a station for them and all other travellers passing that way, and Gus took a heavy toll for meals and feed for stock and even water. In the mountains he had cheap pasturage in the National Forest, for he was an old-timer in the Shinbone Country and had used the grass long before the passage of the act which placed the forest lands under government control. Hence he had the preference, as is the government ruling, and he used it to force out all competing cattlemen in the district.

The war, with the resultant high price of beef and hides, had made him. Ignorant, old, crabbed, alone, unliked by all who knew him, he was now worth nearly half a million dollars, which did him very little good. For he limped about with a cane and had not mounted a horse for several years. Wretched and old and worn to a wreck—and he longed for youth and something to spend his money for, and a bud of a girl named Rosaline Dimmette, who lived with her parents on a forest homestead in the centre of his summer grazing lands.

Until Gus knew the girl he had put forth every effort to oust the homesteaders. But Dimmette was firmly ensconced and had the Agricultural Department back of him; he was obstinate and a fighter. Then one day Gus Tanburt rode up to make further snarling protest against Dimmette's use of the water in a certain stream, and for the first time he saw Rosaline—and wanted her. He decided then and there that the eighteen-year-old girl, fresh and feminine and ruddy as mountain mahogany, should be the price of the Dimmettes' remaining peacefully on their claim. But he knew that he was old and crippled and unacceptable as a husband, and dally growing more so. So the Dimmettes had remained, unhampered by warfare, while Gus Tanburt brooded over his lost youth and vigour and longed for Rosaline.

Then for weeks the papers were full of articles about rejuvenation by the substitution of animal glands in the aged and unambitious. Gus scoffed at it at first, then believed and suffered with longing, then scoffed again. And one day to his rancho came two old acquaintances, Smith Morley and Omar Leach.

Leach, Morley and his wife, after deserting Charmian's expedition on the desert, had ridden back to Diamond H and tried to get possession of at least one of the automobiles. One or both they meant to sell before the party could overtake them, and with the money flee to Australia, where they might have enough funds remaining to outfit themselves for an opal-prospecting trip into the sandy wastes. But Roger Furlong, owner of Diamond H, knew Leach and Morley of old, and knew nothing good about them. He positively refused to turn over to them the cars of Andy and Dr. Shonto, well knowing that the prospectors could not afford such cars. Furlong had recovered his horses and given the two men the boot, but promised to board Mrs. Morley until such time as he found it convenient to take her to the main line of travel to the nearest city. Obliged to be content with this arrangement, Leach and Morley had set out afoot for Tanburt's ranch. They would be more welcome there, for in the past they had turned several shady deals—mostly connected with salted mines and unbranded calves—which had helped to lay the groundwork for the fortune that old Gus possessed to-day. Yes, they might be given a grudging welcome at Tanburt Ranch while they were looking about for a way to get out of their present difficulties. And they reached old Gus at a time when the newspapers, which he read with one thick, dirt-calloused finger pointing out the lines, were carrying columns about the rejuvenation of human glands.

And Gus learned that one of the most famous gland specialists in the world was then on the desert, not many miles away. So with bleary eyes watering in eagerness and trembling hands, he offered to reward Leach and Morley handsomely to find Dr. Inman Shonto and bring him to Tanburt Ranch.

"But how can we go about it?" Leach asked Morley when they were alone. "We can't approach Doctor Shonto after ducking our nuts the way we did. Confound that Shirttail Henry!"

"There's enough in it," said Morley, "to make a trial worth while. We need the money, and it's no time to let our pride stand in the way. Just sneak back and confess we're crooked, and put it up to Shonto what Gus wants. Tell him there'll be a big fee, and— Oh, we'll get by some way! Sufficient to the day is the evil thereof. I can talk better on the spur of the moment than I can after a careful rehearsal."

"Will Shonto come?"

"That's a question. He's got piles of money. He's stuck on Mrs. Reemy. Chances are he won't."

Leach grew thoughtful. "D'ye suppose they're still out there on the desert? What would they be doing, Smith? By now Shirttail Henry has spilled the beans about the opal claims. Chances are they're on their way back to Diamond H right now to get their cars."

"Doubt it. That girl was crazy to find the undiscovered valley, and if they pump Henry he'll tell 'em which way to go to find it. She's game, that kid—be just like her to strike out this late in the season to find it. And the two men would go with her—one to watch the other. They're both in love."

"If that's the case, it'll be harder than ever to find 'em. And harder than ever to get Shonto to come. But if we can find 'em, and can get Shonto off alone, there's a way to get him."

"Of course," Morley agreed pleasantly. "But it'll cost Gus several times what he's offered. And it might be possible to bring Doctor Shonto here by night, or blindfolded, and take him away the same, so he won't know afterward where he was. That'll clear Gus and us, too. And we can arrange to make a getaway by leaving Shonto somewhere on the desert without a horse, so we can ride off and be on our way to Frisco before he gets in touch with anybody."

"Of course," said Leach.

"Let's put it up to Gus how difficult the job will be for us," suggested Morley. "Confound him, he ought to pay us a thousand apiece and never miss it! And say—if we can get Shonto the way we said, we'll get out of crawling back to those folks and making monkeys out of ourselves. That's the best way to pull it off, anyway—and there'll be more in it. If we can only locate the party and get Shonto off by himself. How soon d'ye think they'll be trailing back, Omar, provided they make a try at locating the undiscovered valley?"

"They won't be giving up yet," thought Leach. "But they will before long, I guess. Let's see what Gus'll do for us, then get a couple of horses and a couple of canaries and get back into that country. We can fool 'round and pretend to be prospecting close to the trail to Shirttail Bend. They'll likely come out that way. We can plan the rest of it when we strike 'em."

"Fine business! Let's get to work on Gus and see how much we can separate him from."

The morning following this dialogue Leach and Morley set off over the desert toward the trail that led to Shirttail Bend, mounted and with two packed burros.

They camped near the spring in the calico buttes, and every day they were out merely loafing about, but keeping in sight of the mouth of Henry's trail. But many days had passed before they saw another human being; and they waylaid the first they saw coming down the trail—Shirttail Henry with Lot's wife, on their way with sorrowful news for the Weather Bureau concerning the masticated rain gauge.

From a distance Henry looked at them doubtfully and with long strides tried to evade them. But they closed in on him because of the reluctance of Mrs. Lot to make greater speed than that prescribed for general pack travel. Henry swung flutteringly about and grinned at the prospectors through his mat of ragged whiskers.

"Now, looky-here, you fellas," he threatened. "Come any o' yer monkey-business on me and I'll get a club, and I'll take it and I'll knock yer gysh-danged heads off! Heh-heh-heh!"

This in the face of the fact that there was not a club within fifteen miles.

"Close your trap!" growled Smith Morley. "Where's the bunch?"

"None o' yer gysh-danged business!" was the retort.

"Don't rub his fur the wrong way," came Leach's whispered warning to his partner. "Get more out of him by kidding him along."

Morley tacked. "What's the big idea of being so sore, Henry?" he asked cheerfully.

"Why ain't you boys gone from here?"

"Well, we're just still here—that's all. Prospecting a little. Where you headed for, Henry?"

"Say something about the weather," whispered Leach.

"How's the weather up in the mountains, Henry?" Morley complied. "Looks a little like rain, don't it?"

Henry's blue eyes brightened. "It sure does," he agreed, casting an anxious look at the sky above the wooded ridges. "And here's me without a rain gauge. Plumb ruint, boys. Roger's bell burro she clean et her up. And here's winter comin' on, and me without a gauge! I'm hikin' to Diamond H to send a letter for another one. If I don't get her before it storms I'm plumb ruint—heh-heh-heh!"

His face was so forlorn and his deep-throated chuckle so indicative of secret mirth that the result was ludicrous.

"When'd that happen, Henry?" Leach questioned, affecting interest and sympathy.

"Little time back."

"Where? At Shirttail Bend?"

"No, up above the lake. Furder ner that—up on th' toes o' Dewlap."

"What were you doing up there, Henry?"

"I was showin' 'em how to get to the Valley of Arcana, which is her new name," Henry divulged. "And Roger Furlong's bell burro she—"

"That was sure tough luck, Henry. And did they get to the valley?"

"I don't know. I reckon not. I hadta leave 'em and send in for another rain gauge."

"You ditched them up in that God-forsaken country—a bunch of greenhorns?"

"What could I do?" pleaded Henry. "I'm a gov'ment official, and—"

"Are they up in there yet?"

"I guess so. Ain't seen hide ner hair of 'em since. Left th' hosses at th' lake, and we hoofed it with th' asses. Then, side o' Dewlap, we leaves th' asses browsin' off th' bresh—"

"Yes, yes!"—irritably from Morley. "And you're sure they've not come out?"

"How could they yet? I been hikin' straight sence I left 'em, 'ceptin' to ketch up Mrs. Lot."

"Well, well, well, Henry! Tough luck about your gauge. Don't let us keep you."

"Tough luck, you bet!" Henry agreed. "Heh-heh-heh!"

He slithered to Lot's Wife, who had wandered from the straight and narrow in search of dry bunchgrass, and shooed her into the trail again.

"What'll we do now?" asked Leach. "Go up after 'em or wait here?"

"They'll be coming out soon, with Henry gone," said Morley. "Bet the old coot ditched 'em in the night. If that's so, they'll give up in a day or two. Le's wait for 'em here."

They continued to wait for days and days, anxious, afraid that the party had perished in the wilderness, afraid that Henry had lied to them. Henry had not returned; they supposed he was waiting at Diamond H for the arrival of his new rain gauge, and they knew that mail came to the desert ranch infrequently and at irregular intervals. Morley left Leach on guard and rode back to Tanburt for fresh supplies. He returned, and they continued their patient vigil.

Then one afternoon at three o'clock Dr. Inman Shonto came riding down the trail, alone. They flattened themselves on the ground behind sagebrush and elbowed each other in the ribs in silent satisfaction. Shonto must needs camp at the desert spring that night.

When horse and rider were a mere speck in the hazy distance the prospectors hurried to a draw in which their saddle animals were picketed and raced in a great circle toward the buttes. They rounded the buttes and entered them from the opposite side. They galloped to the spring, collected their belongings, and erased all evidences of a recent camp. They watered their sweating horses and rode out on the desert again, found their pack animals and picketed them, then made a dry camp to await the coming of night.

CHAPTER XXIII
OLD ACQUAINTANCES

IT was one of those Augean tasks that at least once in a lifetime confront all earth-dwellers. But Mary Temple of the lustreless eye and the wispy hair was game to the very core. Dr. Shonto never knew how she suffered from that broken rib throughout the weary days of climbing and sliding back to the haunts of men. Most women suffer silently, and in some ways Mary Temple was a super-woman. She knew, and Dr. Shonto knew, that the broken rib could not mend under the strain that was put upon it. It was an ordeal of pain and torment which must be undergone, and Mary underwent it, acidulously cheerful, barkingly good-natured, a crusty good fellow from the bitter beginning to the bitter end. "Let the old thing hurt," she said. "What's the difference? You get used to pain in time. Our lives are all pain, but we don't know it. We're used to it. When we get to heaven we'll wonder how we ever stood it here on earth, we were so miserable and didn't know it."

This odd philosophy carried her through triumphantly to the lake, where they found the burros and horses still content with their mountain pasture.

To ride, she discovered, was more painful than to walk. So she dragged herself on down to Mosquito and scolded the doctor every step of the way because he insisted on walking with her and leading the saddle horse on which he was to ride for help. At Mosquito, after the terrific strain of days of struggling over the rugged ridges, she collapsed and was put to bed, greatly to her disgust. "I'm a regular zingwham," she sighingly announced. And questioned: "A zingwham is a fat girl thirteen years old that bawls when the boys call her 'Pianolegs.'" And Shonto, days behind because of the slow progress made, hurried his horse on to Shirttail Bend, to find the chaotic ranch deserted by its owner.

Inman Shonto himself was about all in. As medical adviser to as obstinate a patient as any he had dealt with, he had not permitted Mary to carry a pound. (The ensuing argument over this, from the dismal cañon to Mosquito, had helped in his unstringing.) Rations had been short beyond the cache, and at that he had packed a torturing load. His back and shoulders ached; every muscle in his big body ached. His brain was leaden. The figure that camped for the night at the spring in the desert buttes did not closely resemble the fastidious Dr. Inman Shonto, unresponsive but idolized lady's man, renowned gland specialist, popular clubman of the City of Los Angeles.

It was with little zest that he collected petrified yucca for his campfire, fed rolled barley to his horse, and picketed him. Squatting over the coals, he fried bacon and made "cowboy's bread" in the grease. A cup of strong black coffee finished his meal. Not ten minutes afterward he was rolled in his blankets.

For a little his dull senses were aware of the close-by maudlin laughter of a pair of coyotes up in the buttes; then the sounds blended with his dreams and he was fast asleep.

He awoke with a start, shook his head, sat up straight. He was vaguely aware that he was not alone. The fire had died down and only the light of the stars served to reveal several indistinct bulks blacker than the general blackness of the night. He made an attempt to spring to his feet, but found his legs unresponsive and toppled over on one elbow.

A chuckle offered him derisive applause. "They're tied together, Doctor," said a faintly familiar voice. "I just rolled the blankets off your feet and tied your ankles, and you didn't move a muscle."

"Morley, eh?" said the doctor calmly. "Well, Morley, what's it all about? Sore about something—you and your partner?"

"Not at all," Morley replied. Then to Leach: "Stir up the fire and let's have a cup of coffee before we start."

Another dark bulk moved from the collection of shadows, and now Shonto realized that horses and burros comprised the greater part of the group. The fire blazed up after a little, and objects became more distinct.

Smith Morley squatted on his heels.

"I'll tell you, Doc," he said. "Leach and I are up against it. We're flat broke and miles from our headquarters. In you we've found an opportunity to get out of our difficulties. So you're the goat."

"Well, let's have it. Am I to be shot at sunrise or as soon as we've had the coffee?"

Morley chuckled. "I admire your nerve, Doc. You're pretty much of a man, all in all. But if you're worrying any at all, which I doubt, I'll relieve your mind at once. Nothing serious is going to happen to you. We just want you to go with us and perform one of your famous operations on an old desert rat that wants pepping up a little so he can take unto himself a girl-wife. There's a big fee in it for you and a nice little sum for Leach and me to get out of the country on."

"Oh, a friend of yours?"

"Well, 'friend' is a pretty comprehensive word, Doc. Anyway, we've known him a good many years."

"Well," said Shonto, after a brooding pause, "I'm sorry, but I haven't time to perform any operation just now. I'm about the busiest man in the Shinbone Country, I imagine, so you'll have to excuse me. Later, perhaps."

"Just as sorry as you are, Doc, but that's not the way it's scheduled to come out. Leach and I might have put the matter up to you in an ordinary way if we hadn't seen you riding down the trail alone to-day. We realize that the rest of your party must be in trouble somewhere up there in the mountains, and that you're probably going for help. So we decided you wouldn't listen to reason—and tied your ankles. Sorry to disappoint your friends, but you're going with us."

"I'm afraid you're mistaken," was Shonto's brief reply.

"No, not in the least, Doctor Shonto. You're up against a stacked deck. We've got your gun, of course, and, though I suspect that you're a pretty tough *hombre* in a hand-to-hand mix-up, you can't do much with your ankles tied together. So just be reasonable and make the best of it, and you'll be free the sooner."

"Humph!"

Dr. Shonto sat upright, thinking. Morley smiled as he noted the feet constantly twitching and straining under the drab blankets.

"I'll tell you," said Shonto presently. "Things *are* in a pretty serious state up in the mountains. A man's future, if not his life, depends on my getting back to him in time. I'll compromise with you: I'll give you my word of honour that, if you'll let me go and attend to what I have in mind, I'll come back and perform whatever operation your man wants, charge him nothing, and forget the entire matter."

"Sounds good," Morley replied. "And I don't want you to think for a minute that we doubt your word, Doctor. But we're in a desperate hurry. My wife is in hock, you might say, at Diamond H Ranch. Leach and I are stripped. The season's late for prospectors, and we've got to get on our feet at once. We're going to Australia on the money we get out of this, and it's a long trip. Delays are dangerous. No, you'll have to go with us to-night and get it over with. It won't take long, I guess. You'll be on your way again in no time."

"I'll add as much as you're to get from your client for this kidnapping," offered Shonto, "if you'll postpone it."

"That's tempting," admitted Morley, "but this is one of those times when a bird in the hand is worth two in the bush. No, it'll be weeks, maybe, before you're ready. Leach and I can't hold out that long. As it is, we'll be on the briny days before you'd be ready. No, Doc, to-night's the night."

"I haven't an instrument with which to perform any sort of operation," Shonto protested. "You don't seem to realize that an operation of any sort whatever is a delicate piece of business. I need a nurse, a table, anæsthetics, the equipment that a first-class hospital provides—you don't know anything at all about it."

Leach spoke up from the fireside: "This old bird is tough, Doc. All you'll have to do is scrape off the dirt and cut into 'im. Several steers have operated on him already, and bad horses have broken half a dozen bones for him. He can do without the fixings, I guess."

"Well, some things are absolutely necessary," said Shonto. "You'll admit that. And I can't see—"

"Just leave all that to us, Doc," Morley put in. "We'll take you to him, then you can give us a message to wire to Los Angeles, or wherever your headquarters are located, and I'll send it in. Have all you'll need in a couple of days, at most."

Leach approached with two cups of half-cooked coffee.

"Better swallow a cup, Doc," he suggested. "Brace you up for a long night's ride."

Five minutes later, quite unexpectedly, Leach, who had passed behind Dr. Shonto, dropped the noose of a lariat over his head, binding his arms to his sides. The prospector took several turns about his body and made a knot. Then the two unbound the doctor's ankles and helped him to his feet.

Whereupon the struggle began.

Shonto was a powerful man and a determined man. He had small hopes of winning, but there was always a chance and he made the most of his strength. Unable to use his hands, nevertheless he whipped about, butted with his head, tripped with his feet, turned and squirmed, and hurled himself into the kidnappers until the three were about the busiest men in several counties.

But the outcome was inevitable. The lariat did not loosen, and Shonto's huge hands did not come into play. Time and again they bore him to the ground, and, eventually, by reason of one of them having rested while the other engaged the rebellious prisoner, they wore the doctor down. Utterly exhausted, he remained passive while they lifted him to the back of his own horse and confined his ankles again by passing a rope from one to the other under the animal's belly. Then they mounted, urged the burros forward, and, with Morley leading the doctor's horse and Leach riding behind to see that nothing happened, they struck off down the line of buttes. Out on the open desert, they headed into the southwest in the direction of Tanburt's Ranch.

CHAPTER XXIV
MARY CHOOSES A SEAT

DR. INMAN SHONTO was a prisoner in a little adobe hut back of the corrals at Tanburt's Ranch. The dun walls were a foot in thickness, the door of solid slabs of oak securely bolted, and the lone window was less than ten inches square. This hut had once been used as a place to keep milk and butter cool, and in that day was adjacent to the first house that Gus Tanburt had built on his property. The old house had been wrecked in time and a new one built, but the old adobe buttery had withstood the years.

There was no escape; the thick walls and tiny window made imprisonment therein effectual. Shonto paced the floor, smoked his pipe and cigarettes, and tried to hold his temper. He had written the message, and either Leach or Morley had gone with it to the nearest telegraph station. A day and a night had passed, and Shonto had seen nobody but a halfbreed cowpuncher, who brought his meals regularly and thrust them in through the ten-inch opening. He had blankets and a couch, and was fairly comfortable. But, with the exception of the halfbreed, no one paid any attention to him.

He smiled bitterly as he paced about, strong hands clasped behind his back. Up in the mountains a young man soon would be facing a grinning spectre that threatened to ruin his life, and the girl who loved him would be looking on in horror, unable to save him, forced to witness the ghastly thing that was taking place before her eyes. Close at hand an ignorant old man waited for the doctor to perform a trifling operation that promised renewed vigor and the semblance of youth, which would place at the mercy of his selfish desire a ripe girl-woman, pulsing with the warm springtime of maturity.

He had not yet set eyes on this old gargoyle of a man, but he pictured him uncouth, cunning, repulsive, terrifying, as he gloated over his defenceless and shrinking prey. What right had this old monster to demand of life the replenished fires of youth which he had quenched in the soul-warping fight for wealth? Was it consistent with progress that this old man, because he had the means, should be allowed to regain his physical vigour, and perhaps perpetuate his kind in a world already hampered with such as he? Sheep glands substituted for his own worthless organs would not serve to purge his corroded soul nor wipe from his fading mind the cobwebs of superstition and ignorance and prejudice that put him out of step in the march of progress. Such as he should be left to die and be forgotten; it seemed a crime to help him to perpetuate himself, and bring into the world stupid offspring handicapped by heredity from the very start! No, the hope of progress lay in new blood. Let the old generation, with its ignorance and its out-of-tune ideas, become extinct. Let science better the youth of the age, if possible, but refrain from prolonging the life of that arch enemy of Youth and Advancement—Old Age!

The scientist was not only a strong advocate of birth control, but at times he went even further and longed to see the race die out entirely. This, of course, in his bitterest moments, when he realized what a fiasco man had made of life. War and slavery; disease and pestilence; poverty and greed; the stupidity of Labour and the tyranny of Capital; the arrogance of the Church and the cowardice of thinkers; Science devoted to the problem of disassociating atoms one from another so that the world need not search for new oil and coal fields, but neglecting to discover cures for pyorrhea and catarrh; people suffering for the want of food and clothes in a world filled to overflowing with the necessities of life; the timber on a million hills laid low and wasted in a few short years, and families without shelter for their heads!—why prolong this hideous nightmare of confusion? Let the race die out; let the old world groan once more in the travail of a new upheaval; and when it cooled, let protoplastic man be born again in the slime and begin all over from the bottom!

Then thought of his lifelong work with the glands would soothe him, and his kindly eyes would smile. He never could untwist the brains of the generation with his efforts, he knew, but he could lay a foundation for his successors to build upon.

So Dr. Inman Shonto was a great mind. A pessimist to the core, as are most thinkers who search for the eternal truths, he nevertheless worked for the betterment of what he considered hopeless conditions, and wooed optimism while he worked.

Well, he would perform the operation. The deck was stacked against him. In order to save Youth this time he needs must bow to the whims of cantankerous Old Age. But he would make an effort to save that girl, whoever she might be, from the consequences of this iniquitous passion. He would take her away from her poverty to the city and give her a chance in life—he would take her to Charmian and place her under that influence. He would rob this twitching old David of the ewe lamb that he lusted for!

He had reached the ranch blindfolded. Morley had told him of the rancher's cravings, but he had not divulged his name. When the operation was over and his services no longer needed, he would be taken out on the desert, blindfolded again, and left to find his own way to the nearest habitation. Leach and Morley would direct him, they promised, but would ride away and leave him for their own protection. Well, never mind! (Still pacing back and forth, back and forth.) He would get to the bottom of this thing. He would save that girl!

Two days more had passed. Through the little window Dr. Inman Shonto saw that the desert was overhung with clouds. Up over the mountains they were voluminous and black. He believed that it was snowing up there. Every day, perhaps, the mantle of white was being spread deeper and deeper over the land. The stretch of chaparral between Dewlap Mountain and the Valley of Arcana would become impassable. One could not crawl under the branches with the ground covered with snow; and until the snow had reached a depth of twelve feet one could not snowshoe over the tops. Still no sign of the man who had gone to send the telegram.

Midnight, with Shirttail Henry wrapped in his blankets beside the spring in the calico buttes, and Lot's Wife dozing in the background. Lot's Wife snorted and scrambled to her feet. Shirttail Henry stirred, blinked his mild blue eyes, and sat erect. He felt beside him, assured himself that the new rain gauge was safe, and spoke thus to Mrs. Lot:

"Quit snorin', ass, and go to sleep!"

But as he finished the words he heard the thumping of a horse's feet.

Instantly he flung himself from his blankets and stood in a listening attitude. The burro's twelve-inch ears were nearly touching at the tips and her mouseskin muzzle quivered. Her ears pointed the direction from which the horse was approaching.

"Comin' from th' mountains," mumbled Henry. "Funny time o' night to be hittin' th' trail. One critter."

He stepped lightly to the rocks about the spring and flattened himself in the shadows. The thudding continued, and presently, though he could see nothing because of the blackness cast by a cloudy sky, he knew that the animal was close. A single eye of light peered out from the nest of ashes of his waning fire, enough to convince the newcomer, if the horse bore a rider, that some one was camping at the spring. The horse did bear a rider, for no horse, even though he was an exceptional horse and gifted with speech, would have been so peremptory in his demand:

"I want to know who's camping here. Speak out! Who's here?"

"It's me," came Henry's voice from the shadows.

"Oh, old Marblehead, eh? Are you dressed?"

"Yes'm."

"Then step out here, please, and tell me what's become of Doctor Shonto!"

"You're Miss Mary Temple, ain't you?"

"No, I'm Miss William Jennings Bryan. Come on out! What're you hiding there for? Where's Doctor Shonto? I want to know at once. Talk, you damned quitter!"

Henry came forth and stared at the black bulk that she made in the night. Never before had the mild Henry heard a woman use profanity. He was completely flabbergasted.

"I—I didn't know ye cussed, ma'am," he found himself saying.

"What you don't know about me," snapped Mary, "would give you a college education if you could find it out. I curse when I'm mad, like anybody else does who's got any gumption. I'm a bad woman, Henry Richkirk—and don't you forget it!"

"I'm plumb s'prised, ma'am," he puzzled. "You don't cuss when Mis' Reemy's about, do ye?"

"I don't," barked Mary. "But that's no sign I can't. And when I swear I'm mad. Now poke up that fire and tell me what's become of Doctor Shonto!"

"I ain't seen 'im at all, ma'am," said Henry, stirring the embers and heaping on kindling and stony yucca.

"Don't lie to me!"

"Honest!"

"What are you doing here?"

"I been to town to git me a new rain gauge, ma'am. It didn't come right soon, and I—I waited."

"What town?"

"To Emerald, ma'am—that's sixty miles from Diamond H. And I had to camp here to-night 'cause I was all wore out. I got drunk at Emerald, ma'am, and I'm plumb tuckered. But I oughta be in the mountains. Is it rainin' or snowin' up there?"

"It is. Above Mosquito." Mary was dismounting stiffly. "And Doctor Shonto was due to pass Mosquito two days ago. I ought to be in bed, but I rode out to see what had happened to him. I couldn't find anybody at your place when I got there at dusk, so I rode on down. Now I want to know what's become of Doctor Shonto."

"I can't tell ye, ma'am—honest! But I see Omar Leach and Smith Morley clost to th' foot o' th' trail when I was ridin' outa these here mountains here on my way to Diamond H."

"Leach and Morley? What were they doing? What did they want?"

"They were askin' about you folks," Henry told her. "I don't know what they want."

"I know what they want! They want money! Why aren't they out of this country?"

"I can't tell ye, ma'am. They ain't been to Diamond H sence they went back there after they ditched you folks. They left Smith's woman there, but before I got in she'd went out with Roger Furlong in his buckboard to the railroad. Smith and Omar they'd gone to Gus Tanburt's, Roger said. They're friends o' Gus's."

"Who's Gus Tanburt?"

Henry told her, adding: "That's th' only place they could go to, ma'am. Maybe they thought Gus would get 'em outa th' Shinbone Country. But, then, I see 'em at th' foot o' th' trail to Shirttail Bend, like I told ye. And, ma'am, they was somethin' here in camp here that I noticed when me and Mrs. Lot rambled in this evenin'. Ground all tromped, like they'd been a mix-up."

"And you're positive that Doctor Shonto never got to Diamond H Ranch?"

"Just so—sure, ma'am."

"All right. Get me something to eat, please. My grub's back of my saddle. Make me a little tea. I'm sick, Henry. I've got a broken rib, and riding is killing me. But we'll eat and get on to this Tanburt Ranch. How far is it?"

"Why, ma'am, it's miles and miles! And ye don't know th' way."

"You do, though. I want to know what's happened to Doctor Shonto, and you've got to go along and help me find out."

"But, ma'am, I jest can't. It'll be rainin' in th' mountains in less'n twelve hours. You know I'm a gov'ment official, and—"

"Oh, well—forget it!" exploded Mary. "Make me some tea and I'll ride on alone if you can show me the way."

"But, ma'am—"

"Make me some tea, I said—damn it all!"

While he bustled about, hopeful of ridding himself of her after attending to her temporary wants, she watered and fed her horse rolled barley, then threw off the saddle, examined the animal's back with an expert eye, and put it on the picket rope. Presently she came and sat down on the ground by the fire, cupped her bony chin in one lean hand, and gazed eaglelike into the flames.

"Henry," she said, "guess what I'm sitting on."

Henry wheeled and stared at her in blank amazement. He looked all around her, then advanced the theory that she was sitting on the ground.

"Wrong, Henry," said Mary gloomily. "I'm sitting on your new rain gauge. But don't be alarmed. I'm keeping my weight off it. I won't sit down hard, Henry, unless you persist in refusing to accompany me to Tanburt's Ranch to get on the trail of Doctor Shonto. What do you say, Henry?"

Henry had nothing to say, so he looked worried and cackled his silly "Heh-heh-heh!" At half-past one he was stalking into the night in a southwesterly direction, with Mary Temple riding behind him, tortured by the rolling motion of her walking horse, but enduring silently. The rain gauge was strapped at the front jockey of her saddle, its thin brass ready to be squeezed to uselessness if Shirttail Henry became obstinate.

CHAPTER XXV
THE DEADLY BULL AND THE SILVER FOX

IT was nearly noon the following day when a lone horsewoman rode into the grove of cottonwoods that stood before the ranch house of Gustav Tanburt. No one came out to meet her. A few chickens moseyed about, commanded by a black rooster with a red muffler about his neck and a redder comb, deeply notched. He gave Mary Temple a wall-eyed stare. A young calf, tied to a tree on thirty feet of rope, took the occasion to celebrate Mary's advent by racing round in a circle, carrying its tail as if it were broken in the middle, and ending the performance by encircling several trees with the rope and coming to an enforced, bawling standstill.

Mary dismounted in a spasm of suffering, watered her horse at a dripping trough adjacent to a flow of artesian water from a rusty pipe, lowered the reins over the horse's head, and walked to the painfully small and circumspect veranda. She knocked smartly on a weather-stained door, in which a brown-china knob hung like a loose tooth. Gus Tanburt, for all the riches that had been forced upon him, clave to the familiar relics of his days of haphazard struggling.

Mary knocked twice. A large black-green blow fly buzzed about before her peaked nose, seeming to anticipate the opening of the door. Mary struck at it viciously, not with the flat of her hand but with her bony fist. Mary was in no humour to administer punishment with the flat of her hand. She was in the mood to deliver a haymaker and put her scant weight behind it.

Shuffling footsteps preceded the opening of the door, and Gus Tanburt bleared at her from between wind-stung eyelids.

The eyelids had no lashes, and the skin of the rancher's face was slick and shiny as an ancient scar. His teeth were few and far between—yellow fangs in his yielding gums. The breath of his brown clay pipe nearly asphyxiated his gentle caller.

He glowered at Mary as if she were the tax assessor.

"Where'd you come from?" was his inhospitable greeting.

"I'm riding to Britton," answered Mary. (Shirttail Henry had coached her.) "I wanted to know if I couldn't buy something to eat and a feed for my horse."

"Who are ye?"

"My name is Winifred Allison." (Mary always wished she had been born Winifred Allison. Most of us have pet names that we wish our parents had had the sense to bestow on us. Winifred Allison was Mary's.)

"Where ye from?"

"Fresno."

"I mean jest now."

"Oh! I've been riding through the mountains from Glenning."

"Glennin'! That's a hundred an' fifty miles t'other side o' th' range, woman!"

"I'm not disputing that, man!" Mary snapped back. "I'm telling you that I rode from Glenning here, on my way to Britton. What's the odds? Can you sell me some dinner and a feed of hay for the horse?"

Gus Tanburt looked over her ridgy shoulder and squinted at her horse. For a few moments Mary scarcely breathed. But the watery eyes coasted back to her again, and she knew that the rancher had not recognized the animal as belonging to Diamond H.

"I got nothin' fitten to eat," he told her. "I'm a sick man, an' I'm alone and don't wanta be pestered. Ye c'n put th' brute in th' corral and pitch 'im a couple forkfuls o' hay, if ye want to. That'll be fifty cents. Then if ye c'n find anything to eat in th' kitchen ye're welcome to he'p yerself. That'll be a dollar. Waterin' th' brute is fifty cents, a'g'in. Two dollars in all. Strike ye right?"

"Oh, yes," muttered Mary. "Quite reasonable—especially the water, which is going to waste a barrelful every five minutes."

"Well, this here's a desert country, ma'am, an' us folks that put up with stayin' 'way out here gotta make a livin'. Ye c'n take it or leave it. Funny, though, a woman like you all alone forkin' a hoss from Glennin' to Britton. If it's any o' my business—"

"It isn't," Mary broke in. "Where shall I put my horse?"

He shuffled out and to the corner of the house, where he pointed a crooked finger toward one of the large stables, about which was a tumble-down board corral.

"Put 'im in that corral," he said. "That's th' hoss corral. Keep away from t'other'n, though. It runs 'way back in th' cottonwoods, to where ye can't see, an' I got a bad bull in there. He killed a *cholo* last summer."

"All right," said Mary. "I'll not go near him."

She went to her horse, and, afraid to mount because she would display her awkwardness and probably be forced to explain about the broken rib, led the animal past the rancher toward the corral he had indicated. He stood at the corner of the house and watched her until she had taken down the bars and turned in the horse; but Mary had detected no suspicion in his eyes as they roved appraisingly over the animal, as a horseman's eyes invariably will do. She had walked abreast the horse's shoulder to hide the Diamond H brand. He watched her while she took off the saddle and bridle. But he had disappeared before she came from the stable with the second allotted forkful of fragrant alfalfa hay.

Mary carried this forkful to the corner of the stable farthest from the ranch house, as she had the first. Casting a quick glance over her shoulder, she stepped past the head of her eagerly eating horse and was hidden from the house by the stable. She whipped off her hat and waved furiously to Shirttail Henry, hidden somewhere in that part of the cottonwood grove inhabited by the man-killer bull. This bull, Mary believed, was a myth; for she and Henry had approached the ranch buildings so that this neck of the grove would screen them from the inhabitants. Henry had slunk through the grove on reaching it, and she had ridden by to come out on the road that passed through the ranch. She had seen Henry's broad, bewhiskered face peering out at her from a portion of the grove not far from the stables where she had later found hay for her horse. This meant that Henry had walked the length of the grove parallel with her course along the road, and he had not looked as if he had seen anything of the alleged destroyer.

When she began waving Shirttail Henry at once stepped from behind the hole of a large cottonwood and returned the signal. Hastily she scribbled a message on a piece of paper and, holding it up for her aide to see, slipped it under a batten on the side of the stable. Henry waved his understanding of the pantomime, and Mary hurried back in sight of the ranch house and started walking toward it.

She had written:

This old rooster is a crook. He says there is a fierce bull in the grove where you are. He lies. He wanted to keep me away from the other corral and the buildings near it. I'll keep him busy in the house, while you look into all the buildings and see what you can find out. That bull story convinces me that there's something wrong. Don't be a blundering idiot, now, and make a splatchet of everything.

Five minutes after reading the note Shirttail Henry was clinging with his knees to a rail which he had leaned against the adobe wall under the ten-inch window of Dr. Shonto's prison.

Mary Temple contrived to spend an hour and a half in the ranch house. She fried fresh eggs for herself and made baking-powder biscuits and a cup of tea. Gus Tanburt sat in a decrepit kitchen chair and talked with her while she worked, questioning her about anything and everything of which she knew nothing at all. But Mary's was an inventive mind, and she told him about the new schoolhouse at Glenning and spoke feelingly of the last rites solemnized over the mortal remains of one Dan Stebbins, shoemaker, as mythical as Tanburt's bull. Didn't he know Dan? That was strange. But, then, of course he didn't know a great deal about Glenning. Maybe he knew the Morgan girls? No? Mabel had married the young Baptist minister who had recently come from Ohio; and Ethel Morgan was—well, perhaps the least said about Ethel the better. She had bobbed her hair, though, and he could draw his own conclusions.

When the ordeal was over Mary laid a couple of dollars on a place in the oilcloth-covered table where the oilcloth had not worn off, and thanked the old profiteer in her sweetest manner. Tanburt did not know that Mary's sweetness was inevitably a danger signal, so, refreshed with much fictitious news, he accompanied her to the door in a more agreeable frame of mind and invited her to drop in again if she ever rode through in the future. But he was too miserable to saddle her horse for her, and bade her good-by on the porch.

Tucked under the same batten on the east side of the stable Mary read, on the reverse side of her note:

Doctor is in that little dobe the othir side off the coral. Met me a mile down the rode to the west of tanberts. I left this note before I left.

"There," murmured Mary, "is what you call American efficiency, which I always suspected was pretty much hot air. He left the note before he left. Henry! Henry! if all of our government officials were like you!"

The short winter day was drawing to its close. The sun was sinking slowly behind the Coast Range, having dropped suddenly from under a rack of clouds for its first smile of the day before seeking its bed in the mystic west.

Then two horsemen galloped easily from a short pass through a chain of half-hearted buttes that barely broke the monotony of the level desert on the road from Tanburt Ranch to Britton. The first horse shied and snorted, almost unseating its rider. The second, frightened by the action of the first, reared on its hind legs and wheeled.

An apparition suddenly had confronted the little party. Mary Temple, gaunt and severe of mien, had appeared uncannily in the middle of the road, with a leveled Winchester at her shoulder.

"Up!" she commanded acidly, as the horses came to a dancing halt. "Quick! Climb the ladder, both of you! Don't make a mistake. I've killed my man."

Then the hammer clicked icily as she cocked it in the desert stillness.

That was the master stroke of the whole performance—that ominous click that followed her unimpassioned command. It was psychological. Leach and Morley thrust their hands above their heads and grinned uncomfortably.

"Henry! Morley has a six-gun on his hip. Get it. Morley, let him get it. I'm telling you the God's truth when I say I'll pull the trigger if you move a hand. Damn you, anyway—I'd as soon take a crack at you as break an egg!"

"Wh-why, Miss Temple!" gasped Smith Morley.

"Shocked, eh? Well, if you'd seen me when I ran the Silver Fox Dance Hall in Alaska, ten or eleven years ago, you'd know who you're dealing with. But if you want to take a chance—Henry!"

"Yes'm—here I am."

Henry quivered from behind the large greasewood bush that had concealed him, and, grinning apologetically, stepped to the side of Morley's horse and removed a wooden-handled .45 from its holster.

He heaved a sigh of relief as he backed away.

"Now," he said, "try to come any o' yer capers on me, Smith and Omar, an' I'll get me a club—"

"You'll do nothing of the sort," Mary cut in crisply. "Why not blow their heads off with their own gat?"

"Heh-heh-heh!" chuckled Henry.

"Hit the ground," Mary commanded. "Keep your hands up and turn your backs to me."

Leach obeyed instantly, but a look of disdain had come upon Morley's features as, the first shock over, his courage began welling up again.

"You wouldn't shoot—"

The remainder of his sentence was drowned by the roar of the Winchester, and the prospector felt the wind of the bullet as it crashed past his cheek. There followed the instant clacking of the mechanism as Mary pumped another cartridge into the chamber. The horses lunged and danced.

"You were saying, Mr. Morley?" Mary prompted sweetly.

But Morley was sliding from his plunging horse to the ground, where he carried out to the letter the commands of the erstwhile mistress of the Silver Fox.

"There's some of the doctor's stuff tied behind Leach's saddle," Mary said to Henry. "Get it."

Henry obeyed.

"Tie it behind my saddle," was the next command.

Henry complied.

"Now get on Morley's horse," said Mary; and Henry mounted.

"Take the reins of the other horse and be ready to lead him."

Henry swung Morley's horse to the head of Leach's and took the reins. At the same time Mary was mounting her own animal, and she did it quickly, despite the pain that the jerky movement gave her.

"All right," she said to Henry. "Lead out at a gallop."

Morley risked a glance over his shoulder. "You're not going to leave us 'way out here on the desert, Miss Temple!"

"That's what *you* say," said Mary, and with her hat spanked the rump of the horse that Henry was to lead to stir him into a gallop from the jump.

A clatter of hoofs up the darkening desert road, and Leach and Morley were alone with their thoughts.

Perhaps fifteen minutes later Mary slowed down to a walk, and, racked with pain, sat gasping in her saddle.

"Ma'am," said Shirttail Henry, whose horse had slowed with his mate, "ye're a outlandish uncommon woman. I never guessed ye was th' kind to ever run a dance hall like that Silver Fox place ye told about back there."

"No?" gulped Mary. "Well, I never did—but don't you suppose I ever read a story in my life? You talk too much. My rib hurts like fury. Shut up!"

CHAPTER XXVI
THE LAST TABLET

OVER the Valley of Arcana the snow banners streamed from the mastheads of the surrounding peaks. Snow fell in the valley—soft snow that somehow seemed warm instead of cold. It disappeared on the bosom of the river, but thickened in eddies and made slush against piles of driftwood. The Valley of Arcana had not yet felt the grip of winter, but up above the banners of triumph waved and the artillery of the blizzards boomed.

The Cave of Hypocritical Frogs was comfortable. The cold did not penetrate to its inner recesses. At the mouth Andy kept a fire going, and enough deadwood had been gathered to last all winter.

The snowbound prisoners sat together below the cave, on boulders close to the redwood saplings which made a bridge over the waterfall that told them weird tales of the waste places night and day. Often the speech of the talkative water changed to music, gathered unto itself rhythm and tunefulness. Sometimes choir boys were singing; sometimes male quartets; more often they fancied that ghost women, wild and distraught from woes undreamed of by mortal beings, were wiping their wet, clinging hair from their faces and lifting their voices in a piercing heathen chant of denunciation.

They sat together above the fall and watched the boiling water in the pool below—marvelled over the frenzied happiness of a lone water ouzel that frolicked there.

He stood on a half-submerged stone and danced, this odd diving bird of the riffles and waterfalls, who seems to sing best when the water is cold as ice and dashing over him and about him. He courtesies and nods to right and left and sings happily whether or not the sun is shining; and then he dives. His are the pounding torrents, his the screaming rapids, his the showers of coldest spray that never chill his song. Alone, bobbing—smiling, one almost imagines—he seeks the cold dark cañons where water roars, for dashing sprays are his sunshine. "The mountain stream's own darling, the hummingbird of blooming waters," wrote "Wonderful John" of him—John Muir, lover of God's own!

Hand in hand they sat and watched the ouzel, bobbing and bowing as if pretending to shrink from the plunge he loved, and listened to his misty notes and the changing oratory of the waterfall. They were silent. Both were thinking deeply. For the day before Andy Jerome had swallowed the last half-tablet, and up above the snow was hourly closing the way for Dr. Shonto to come to them with more. Over them hung this thought like the thread-held sword of old.

"Dear," said Charmian, with that little upward twist of her mouth that always made him want to kiss it, "do you know that your beard is growing fearfully long? You see, I'm taking a proprietary interest in you already. What'll I do to you after we're married?"

Andy laughed. "To tell the truth," he replied, "I made a great blunder on this trip. Usually, out in the woods, I carry an old-fashioned razor. But this time I brought along my safety. And every blade is dull as a hoe. Can't sharpen razor blades on sandstone, as I do my axe and knife.

"But wouldn't I be out of character if I failed to grow a beard? Ought to hang down on my manly breast and be full of burrs or something. And you ought to be wearing a knee-length skin dress, with the hair on. I'm afraid we aren't playing up to our rôles properly."

"I'm glad to see you so light-hearted," she observed pensively. "I'm—I'm afraid I'm worrying a little too much, Andy."

His brow clouded instantly, and she knew that his lightness of heart was feigned.

"It *is* storming like the dickens up there," he admitted. "Doctor Shonto will never be able to get through that stretch of chaparral if it continues. And—"

"Yes?" she prompted.

"And I guess it'll continue, all right," he finished gloomily.

The hand that he held trembled a little.

"It wouldn't be so bad," she mused, "if—if— Well, we could live here all winter, I believe. We can get plenty to eat—such as it is—and we can always keep warm. But—"

"Yes, I know." He squeezed her fingers. "It's the devil. If we only knew what to expect! What the dickens is the matter with me, anyway? And why didn't the doctor tell *you*, at least?"

"He explained that—almost. He wants to be fair. He hoped that he could get back in time to save you from—from whatever is to happen to you. Then there would be no need to tell what he knows. He took that chance, do you understand? But now he won't get back in time, and—and we'll soon know what your great trouble is."

She sighed wearily.

"Whatever it is, Charmian, you'll never give me up, will you, dearest?"

"Never!"

They kissed long and tremulously, then the girl rose to her feet and pulled at his hand till he stood beside her.

"Let's go back to the Cave of Hypocritical Frogs," she said. "It's getting cold out here. And see, Andy—the snow is beginning to thicken on the ground. It'll be white by morning."

That same day she was putting their simple belongings to rights in the Cave of Hypocritical Frogs. Each had a table—a flat-topped stone—on which articles of daily use were kept. Womanlike, she fussed over his things, which he consistently left awry. He was outside cutting wood. She cleaned his comb and military brushes and laid things straight, then opened the leather-covered case that contained his safety-razor to make sure that he had not overlooked an unused blade. And in the little metal container she found three, still sealed in their paper covers.

She called to him:

"No caveman stuff for you for a time, young fellow! Come in here! I've found three new razor blades!"

"Good work!" he praised her when he reached her side. "Wonder how I came to overlook 'em. Guess I just took it for granted they were all gone, and didn't open the case at all."

But by next day his beard, which had reached the most unattractive stage, still covered his face.

"Andy, why don't you shave?" she asked.

"By George! Forgot all about it. Getting used to this fuzz, I guess. Maybe I like it—I don't know."

His laugh was insincere, and she regarded him in mild surprise.

They were busy at separate tasks throughout that day, Andy having gone down the river alone to make an effort to get the canoe closer to the cave, and Charmian washing clothes down by the pool below the waterfall. At supper she once more reminded him that he had not shaved.

His boyish face grew red with confusion, and he stammered an apology. The pine cones that they used as torches would not give enough light for shaving after supper, and next morning he tramped away again with the beard still covering his face.

She took him to task again when he returned at noon, standing before him and demanding, with a look of worriment in her eyes, the why of it.

"I—I just don't seem to want to," he confessed. "I don't know why. But I hate to begin. Always dreaded the thing, and out here it seems so unnecessary."

Then it was that she noticed his finger nails, for he had raised one hand to his shaggy beard and was fondling it abstractedly while it was under discussion. His finger nails were long and black with dirt.

"Why, Andy!" she began; then stopped short, her face whitening.

Always Andy had been clean and neat, so far as the conditions of camp life and the trail would permit. In fact, saving Dr. Shonto, she never had known a more fastidious man. Otherwise she never could have considered him her equal. A terrible thought came to her: This sudden shuffling off of the demands of civilization must be the first symptom of his malady. Considerately she said nothing, but for two days watched him closely, her heart like lead. He neither washed nor cleansed his finger nails during those two days, and she imagined that a certain amount of lustre had left his one-time bright-blue eyes.

And then he yawned directly in her face one night, his mouth wide open, with no hand raised to cover the gap and no apology. And two days later she caught him eating broiled meat with his fingers, tearing it apart as if he never had seen a knife and fork.

She cried herself to sleep that night and rose next morning with terror in her heart.

And now the change came fast. Andy's eyes became bleary. The colour of his face grew leaden, and the cheeks were bloated. His skin took on a dirty, flabby look. His tongue, which the horrified girl often saw hanging out at one corner of his mouth, had thickened, and the lips were perpetually moist. His breath became asthmatic. When he spoke he mumbled his words. Gradually, but with cruel swiftness, the light of reason left his leaden eyes; and within ten days after the last tablet had been swallowed Charmian Reemy knew that the man she loved was little better than an idiot.

His head lopped forward as he sat at the mouth of the cave and stared, saying not a word, gazing at nothing, occasionally drawing in his swollen tongue, but never wiping from the ragged beard the saliva which he had drooled upon it. Again the tongue would creep out and downward, as if he lacked the muscular energy to keep it in its place. His long hair hung over his imbecile eyes; his long finger nails, unsightly with dirt, looked like the talons of a bird.

He would rouse himself when she shook him and, with tears streaming down her face, begged him to pull himself together. He would grin at her then and lick his lips with his thick tongue, but in a moment or two he would once more lose control of his faculties, and his head would drop forward, while out would creep the repulsive tongue. Sometimes he would laugh—a weird, insane chuckle that wrenched from the tortured girl a sob half of pity, half of horror. He walked occasionally, but did no work at all. When this occurred he dragged his steps, swaying loosely from side to side as if his body knew no joints. He would pause often and, swaying slightly, would gaze this way and that as if trying to replace in his memory the significance of familiar objects.

A few days more and he had ceased to speak. He muttered now and then, for no particular reason whatever, but his wet lips formed no words. Sometimes he gazed at her as she moved about, but in his eyes was no question as to what she might be doing; the motion of her body simply had attracted him momentarily and aroused a flicker of interest. But it would pass at once, and again he would let his head go forward, and sit gazing at the ground, while his tongue hung out and dripped.

Meanwhile it snowed. The ground was covered two feet deep about the cave. Up in the higher altitudes the blizzards raged perpetually, and the air was filled with dismal moanings. All hope of Dr. Shonto's returning to the Valley of Arcana, except in an aeroplane, had vanished.

And the idiot sat at the door of the Cave of Hypocritical Frogs and drooled, staring through his hanging hair!

Never before had Charmian Reemy known fear, but now she suffered abject terror. All about her was ice and snow, and she shivered when a new note came in the monotonous roar of the waterfall. No longer sang the silver-throated choir boys. The high-pitched chorus that her fancy had once named theirs became the sinfully gleeful giggling of malicious sprites as they triumphed over her great disaster. The rollicking songs that the male quartet had sung changed to the bellowing of Satan, as when the angel of the Lord came down from heaven with the key to the bottomless pit and chained him for a thousand years. Wrapped in her blankets, nightmares came to her so that she was afraid to sleep without the flickering light of a pine knot near her. Often she awoke screaming, gripped by an icy, throat-contracting fear. And once the nightmare took upon itself reality—and Madame Destrehan's prophecy was fulfilled.

There were fingers at her throat, long, curving talons that were black with dirt. Maniacal eyes looked into hers through a screen of hanging hair. Wet lips were close to her face, seen through a mat of unkempt beard, and from them lolled a tongue, black and swollen.

She thought that she fainted—she did not know. But for a space of time—how great she never knew—the flickering pine-knot torch was gone and an icy wave swept over her. Then she was up, shrieking, struggling madly, hers the strength of half a dozen women. She hurled the ogre away from her, striking, clawing, pushing, and it crashed against a wall of the cave and sank to the floor in a disorderly heap.

Panting, one hand clutching her breast, she gazed at it, huddled there, inert, breathing asthmatically. Then it moved, half rose, reclined once more in a posture more human and natural.

For an hour she watched, while the cold pierced her bones. Then, mustering her courage, she stole past IT to the outer chamber of the cave, where she collected blankets, brought them back, and threw them over the prostrate figure of what once had been Andrew Jerome. With her own blankets wrapped about her she remained in a sitting position, stark awake, until the cold, feeble light of another day in the Valley of Arcana crept in.

He was not injured. He merely had lost in a twinkling the brief flicker of energy that had returned to him, perhaps in a dream. Perhaps he had been asleep throughout, and his subconscious mind had revived and energized him where his conscious mind had failed to function. Perhaps her fierce defence had awakened him and had caused him to lapse back. He dragged himself up when it was light, and she guided him to his customary seat at the mouth of the cave.

Her daily needs served eventually to turn her mind on necessary tasks, which helped her to forget the horror of her days and nights. She must conserve the jerked meat, which together they had smoked so carefully over the smouldering fires, and attend to the traps. She trudged away through the snow, forced to leave Andy to his fate, gaping there at the mouth of the Cave of Hypocritical Frogs. But when she reached the first dead-fall and found a dead jackrabbit beneath the fallen stone she let it lie. One by one she visited other traps, springing them when she found no little dead body, and releasing live quail caught in the quail traps. She would eat the jerky, and when that was gone— Well, then she would find something else. She could not kill!

Sometimes she was almost tempted to pray that something might happen to Andy—that he might rouse himself and try to wander somewhere through the rocks, and meet with a fall that would end in instant death. He was almost helpless. She had brought herself to wash his hands and face, shuddering with repulsion, and whacked off the offensive claws. She wanted to shave him, but was afraid that she did not know how, and shrank from the task. As yet he was able to feed himself, but in a manner that was wolfish when it was not like the food-cramming of a two-year-old; and she turned her back and never ate with him. The firewood was plentiful, and she had only to cut it or break it with the hunter's axe. All day long she kept the smoke of the signal fire streaming aloft, but she imagined that it was dispersed by the blizzards sweeping overhead, and would serve no purpose even were the doctor trying to reach her.

She cut wood and washed clothes, pulverized nuts and acorns for bread, cooked their meals, and watched the snow pile up about the Cave of Hypocritical Frogs, and when there was nothing to do she left her charge and sought the waterfall, unable to bear the pitiable sight of him. Not that there was solace in the roaring and croaking and murmuring of the water. Its icy sheets depressed her immeasurably. But below it played and sang the water ouzel, happy, bobbing up and down and nodding sidewise, singing as if there were no terrors upon the earth, while over him and about him dashed the freezing spray. He who could sing at the top of his voice and dance throughout days that were dull and dreary, in the very teeth of the raging waters, gave solace.

CHAPTER XXVII
ADRIFT ON LOST RIVER

HERE sat Charmian abreast the pounding waters, sobbing at times as if her heart would break, while up at the cave lolled the drivelling thing that once had been a man, young and handsome and pulsing with the thrill of life. The little water ouzel bowed and bobbed to her, perched on a stone in the frothy pool below. He was like a boy stripped for the first spring plunge into his favourite swimming hole, but jouncing on the spring-board, shivering in anticipation of the chilling dive, and thinking up excuses to postpone it. Yet always he dived, broke the surface of the water again, and perched himself once more on his aquatic throne. Here he bobbed his head to the girl and danced about, then lifted a voice attuned to the song of the dashing waters, but merging trills of gladness with their funeral dirge. He was always there; he never failed her. He feared her not at all, neither did he court her. The only jarring element in their companionship was his complete indifference to her presence. But she forgave him this when he sent forth his fluty notes in defiance of ice and snow and driving spray. Here she sat and wept, ofttimes trembling from the cold, and prayed for relief from this hideous thing that had come upon her.

Her brief dream of love had faded. At first she had striven bravely to keep the fires burning, devoting herself to sacrifices for him, trying to remember him as he had been only a few short days before. At times she hated herself for what she considered her inconstancy and lack of character. But her dream of love had gone—and now she realized that love never had existed. He had swept her off her feet, this once handsome, careless boy, and her youth had responded to his. Now she had time to think, and she knew that she had dreamed.

She remembered now how she had tried to draw him into serious discussion of various topics that interested her, and should have interested him, and how persistently he had evaded them. He had been a student of the law, but even upon that topic she had been unable to draw a thoughtful word from him. Light-hearted, boyish, shallow-minded, care-free he had always been, with never a thought for the morrow, his distant future, or hers. How bitterly she recalled all this now! How blind she had been! Never could they have been happy together. She had not loved Andy Jerome—the female in her had succumbed to the male attraction that his vigorous manhood offered; she had surrendered to that alone.

Dr. Shonto had been right. Dr. Shonto was always right. Andy Jerome was not for her. Now she saw that, with this dreadful thing constantly threatening him, his family had not urged him to mental performances which would strengthen his mind and character. Out of love for him they had let him go his way, well supplied with money, and with nothing to bother him. His schooling, she imagined, had been a mere pretence, designed to delude him and his friends into believing he was normal. In the end he would have turned out a failure, perhaps, but he would not have been the first failure in a rich man's family. Nothing would have come of it, and he would have lived his life in blissful ignorance of the real cause of his failure. Dr. Inman Shonto, she believed, had counselled them to do this.

She was thinking of Inman Shonto hourly these days—of his grave, kindly smile, his tolerance of human shortcomings, his knowledge, success, liberal ideas, and lofty idealism. She never once thought of his ugliness of face. In her picture of him she saw only the magnetic smile and the power of that face.

It had occurred to her once—just once—that Shonto might have prolonged his return so that Andy would run out of his medicine, when he would be revealed to her in all his monstrousness. But she had put the ungenerous thought behind her instantly. Dr. Shonto never would stoop to such a thing as that.

No, something serious had detained him. He would come to her soon, if it was possible for an aeroplane to cope successfully with the mountain blizzards that raged over the Valley of Arcana. He would return to her. She heard it in the unceasing song of the little water ouzel.

She had lost track of the days. Andy now was helpless, insensible to cold and pain. At night she helped him to his blankets, made him lie down, and wrapped him up. She slept in the outer chamber of the cave now—slept fitfully, for she must needs be up every other hour to replenish the fire, lest her charge throw off his covering and freeze to death. Also her own covering was insufficient, for it was growing colder, and but for the cave and the leaping fire she surely would have suffered from the steadily lowering temperature.

She rose one morning about nine o'clock. The sky was leaden, as usual, and the wind moaned over the Valley of Arcana. It was cold and dreary in the cave, for she had slept for the past three hours and the fire had died down to a bed of coals. She glanced once at the huddled form under the blankets, then with the wooden shovel moved the drifted snow from the entrance and rebuilt the signal fire outside. Then she made acorn bread—how she hated it!—soaked and stewed jerked rabbit, and laid out on the stone table an array of dried grapes and huckleberries.

When the unappetizing meal was ready she tried to drag the inert man from his blankets, but he muttered and refused to move. So she ate, and afterward made an effort to feed him, but without avail.

She wondered if he was dying. She wondered, too, at her indifference. Surely he would be better dead. Her existence had become a primitive one, and primitive people are wont to look at such things as life and death in a most pragmatic light. But she hated herself again for not worrying over his fate. If he refused to eat, however, what could she do? Dr. Shonto had told her that she would know what to do if the tablets should run out before his return. She knew now what he had meant. She could feed Andy and keep him from freezing—and nothing more!

She left him wrapped in his blankets, breathing huskily, a motionless heap of animal matter. She waded through the snow that had drifted into the trail, which the previous day she had cleared, and sought the waterfall and her friend of the driving spray.

He was there before her, perched upon his stone, bowing and scraping, and bobbing about like a hard working auctioneer. This morning, however, his song failed to cheer her. She wondered if she were going mad. Strange thoughts had been in her mind since she had arisen. She somehow seemed indifferent to what might lie before her. She was dull and apathetic, and it seemed that she almost was as insensible to grief and fear as that vegetated man lying like a dying fish in the Cave of Hypocritical Frogs. She could not cry this morning. With dull eyes she gazed at the antics of the water ouzel, and her thoughts were taken up with a vague wonder of everything—life particularly. She wondered who she was, why she was, what she was—wondered if her past were all a dream—wondered if she had not lived in this deserted valley always, and only dreamed of civilization and a girl called Charmian Reemy.

She must fight this off. She was growing afraid—afraid of herself! She twisted her fingers together in a sudden agony of realization of her plight, as when an unannounced wave of understanding sweeps across the befuddled mind of a drunken man and he knows that he is drunk, and for a moment suffers deep remorse. She rose to her feet to walk about for warmth—

And then the water ouzel bobbed to the surface and flew to his perch; and near the place where he had risen she saw a shining object tossing about in the writhing current.

It was such an unfamiliar object that she stood and looked at it uncomprehendingly. It was about a foot in length, seemed cylindrical, and was unaccountably bright. This brightness had attracted her. It was so out of place in that dull-coloured land.

It was a length of tree limb, she told herself. Some piece of driftwood twelve inches long by three inches in diameter, with the bark slipped off. But what had made the under bark so bright? Was it river slime?

Certainly—it could be nothing else.

She turned away, stopped—turned back again.

There it was eddying about in the swirling water. It was bright! Bright! Bright like metal! And metal did not float—

Except!

With a new strange thought she clambered rapidly down over the stones and reached the level of the ouzel's throne. She found a long stick, but it was far too short to reach the queer object tossing upon the boiling water. She watched it tremblingly. It *was* metal. No inner bark could assume that brightness, no slime of the water could cause a piece of limb to deceive the eye so easily.

All eagerness, fearful of disillusionment, she tested the water's depth, but had known before she did so that she dared not venture in.

The riotous current, twisting this way and that without stability of direction, had swept the bright object to the middle of the pool once more. And now it struck the main channel and went racing downstream, past the water ouzel's perch, and into the straight stretch of river below.

And Charmian knew that it was of metal and meant for her.

The lost river! Down Lost River, through the mysterious underground passages, Dr. Inman Shonto had sent a message to her, incased in a metal cylinder!

Feverish with anxiety, she clambered over the stones and reached the level land above the pool. Now, running with all her might, she followed the river's course through the heavy snow. The metal cylinder was being swept downstream at a rapid rate. Her only hope lay in reaching the canoe ahead of it, and paddling out to await its coming.

Trees and boulders shut off her view of the river. Hence she had no notion of the speed of the drifting cylinder, and in greatest excitement and dread of loss she waded on through the drifts, streaming perspiration. Almost the last rational act of Andy Jerome before he succumbed to the hideous malady had been to paddle the canoe upstream as near as possible to the cave. He had been obliged to beach it below a second waterfall, past which the two of them had been unable to carry it.

At last, staggering on, she heard abreast of her the roar of the lower waterfall. She left the open and ploughed into the trees. She reached the river, staggering from the fierce strain. And now a dread thought came to her: Had she the strength to shove the heavy, awkward craft into the water? She remembered that it had required the combined efforts of her and Andy to launch it before, to which they had found it necessary to add no little ingenuity.

But a feeble cry came from her lips as she neared the spot where they had left it. The river had risen. The canoe had launched itself and was riding easily at the end of the tough grass rope that they had braided for a painter and tied to a sapling on the river bank.

She had never paddled this canoe, nor any other canoe. She knew, though, from what Andy had told her, that she must be cautious and not unbalance the clumsy craft. In her excitement she had stepped into it, taken up the paddle, and propelled it to the limit allowed by the grass rope before she realized that it was still made fast to the sapling.

She pulled inshore again and stepped out, when, as she fumblingly untied the rope, she realized that it would be folly for her to paddle to the middle of the stream until the cylinder came in sight. She would wait inshore in the canoe, with paddle in readiness, until she saw the bright object coming down on the swift current.

She carefully entered once more, and knelt on the rough bottom with her crude paddle. And now the terrible idea seized her that perhaps she had been too slow and that the cylinder had long since drifted by.

She waited, torn by doubt and indecision, and was on the point of leaving the canoe and plunging on downstream when a bright something came toward her bobbing on the waves in the middle of the river.

With an inarticulate cry she shoved off and paddled awkwardly ahead of it. Then the main current caught her, whirled her completely around, and started her downstream at the same rate that the cylinder was travelling.

She paddled upstream, but seemed unable to gain a foot. She dipped more vigorously, her eyes on the drifting object of her hopes. The canoe was swept into a rapids, struck a snag—and next instant she was in the icy water, with the canoe capsized and hurrying on.

She could swim, and her bellows breeches did not impede the movements of her legs as a skirt would have done. But she wore her heavy hiking shoes; the current was swift and dangerous; the river was deep; in a deplorably short time the ice-cold water would chill her blood and benumb her muscles.

She struck out bravely; but, already half exhausted from her race through the snowdrifts, she made little headway toward the snag that had capsized the canoe. The water boiled over her, swept her about unmercifully, and blinded her. Terror seized her as she realized that she was not equal to the struggle against it. She went completely under three times, twisted down by the undertow or whirlpools. She was losing! She could not make the snag.

And then, coming up for the fourth time, gasping for air, her outflung hand touched something hard and smooth, and her fingers closed over a cylinder of brass.

Five minutes later, stunned, almost unable to move a limb from the deadly coldness of the water, she half swam, half floated to a projecting rock far downstream from the point where she had grasped the cylinder. She clutched it with a hand, rested a minute or more, then dragged herself upon it and lay gasping for breath, with the cylinder pressed to her heaving breast.

CHAPTER XXVIII
THE MESSAGE

CHARMIAN was more dead than alive, as the saying goes, when she reached the Cave of Hypocritical Frogs. Here, with shaking hands, she stripped to the skin and rubbed her limbs and body as vigorously as her benumbed condition would permit, her teeth chattering like a tiny riveting machine. The signal fire was smouldering. She raked away the green conifer branches which kept the smoke stream rising and heaped on dry wood. It blazed up soon, and when she dared she stood close to it invoking its warmth.

An hour had passed before she felt able to examine the brass cylinder that had come floating so mysteriously down the ice-fringed river.

As has been stated, it was about a foot in length by three inches in diameter. One end was solid brass. The other end had been sealed with brown wax.

Huddled close to the fire, nude but for the blanket that was wrapped about her, she hacked tremblingly at the wax, first with a hunter's axe and then a jackknife.

The wax surrendered to her prying, and she hacked out perhaps two inches of it. It had been poured in to this depth, she reasoned, to guard against its being loosened by stones and sticks against which it might have bumped in its underground passage from the mountains above the valley.

At last it was all loose. She dumped the last of it on the cave floor. Looking in the cylinder, she saw a pasteboard disc the exact size of the container, which had been pressed down against the cargo of this mysterious carrier to stand as a partition against the contents and the melted wax.

She pried it out with the point of her knife as one fishes for an obstinate cork. Then, holding her breath, she poured the contents of the cylinder on the floor.

Small paper bundles fell out, and among them was a folded piece of paper. This she grasped up first, unfolded, and found to be a note signed Inman Shonto. She read, while the tears brimmed in her eyes:

"MY DEAR CHARMIAN:

"This is the fourth brass cylinder that I have thrown in Lost River in the hope that it will float through the underground passages to the Valley of Arcana, where you may find it. A note accompanied its three predecessors, and each one instructed you to build two signal fires if you found the cylinder so that I would know it had reached you. For several days I have watched the stream of smoke from your fire, longing always to see the second stream ascend. And I have suffered because no second stream came.

"I have about decided, therefore, that Lost River does not run through the valley, or that my cylinders have caught on something and failed to reach you. For in some strange way it seems to me that, if they did float into the Valley of Arcana, you would find them. Which is childish of me, I suppose. But it bolsters up my courage nevertheless. I have only three more cylinders to send, and will send them two days apart unless I see the second stream of smoke.

"Now follows a repetition of what the other messages contained:

"Build another signal fire as soon as you have read this, so that I will know you have received my message and are again in command of the situation. By this time, I think, Andy Jerome will have lapsed into a terrible state, and you will be almost insane. But in the cylinder you will find more tablets. Give him one a day regularly—no more—and if he is not too far gone he will come back to normalcy with surprising swiftness. It may seem incredible to you, but it is the truth.

"Andy Jerome, Charmian, is a cretin. A cretin, you perhaps must be told, is an hereditary idiot. Cretinism is most prevalent in the Swiss Alps, where Andy's ancestors lived—on his mother's side, I mean. Up until recently cretinism has been considered incurable by the medical profession; but the discovery that man is regulated by his gland secretions had done away with that theory. Cretins are only human beings suffering from a lack of thyroid in their systems. Their other glands may be functioning properly, but when the secretions of the thyroid are deficient they are hopeless idiots. However, science has discovered that if they are fed daily a tablet composed of the extract of the thyroid glands of sheep they will, to all intents and purposes, become normal. But in a few days after the treatment is stopped they will quickly slip back into cretinism again, with all its degradation. Then let the treatment be renewed, and in a short while the patient will have lost all of the symptoms of cretinism and gradually will come back. It seems incomprehensible, I realize, but it is nevertheless a thoroughly demonstrated scientific fact.

"Cretinism runs in Andy's family. Certain children of a generation ago in his mother's family were born cretins. Others escaped to a certain extent. Andy's mother, for instance, is perfectly normal in every way. But the taint cropped up in her child when he was about eight years of age, at which time I was working hardest on my theory regarding the significance of the gland secretions as determinants of human personality. I myself brought Andy out of cretinism and made him appear like other men.

"We have been careful with him and have encouraged an outdoor life. While he seems to learn readily, he takes no particular interest in his studies, is irresponsible, and unsettled in his habits. He has never missed a day in taking his medicine, for I refused to experiment with him. I am not sure now that he has lapsed back into cretinism; but, considering the time that I have been away, it seems almost certain that he should be pretty far gone.

"My delay in returning to you was unavoidable. I think that I could have made it back ahead of the snows if I had not encountered our old friends Leach and Morley, who kidnapped me, blindfolded me, and led me into a series of strange adventures."

Here followed a brief account of the doctor's imprisonment in the adobe hut at Tanburt Ranch and of his subsequent release by Shirttail Henry and Mary Temple.

"Marvellous Mary Temple!" continued the letter. "Suffering agonies because of her broken rib, she nevertheless refused to give in until she and Henry had ridden to the ranch, after her spectacular hold-up of the prospectors, and set me free. Old Gus Tanburt was mooning about the house, I guess, and we got away from the ranch after dark with little difficulty. Then I relieved Shirttail Henry of his horse—or, rather, Tanburt's horse—and Mary and I rode all night to Diamond H Ranch. Henry, I suppose, walked back to his camp in the buttes, with fifty dollars that I gave him for another drunk. He said he had spent all of the two hundred and fifty that you gave him for his services as guide. Poor old Henry! Mary says one more hot day will finish him!

"At Diamond H we got my car and I drove Mary to the city, where I rushed her to a hospital and commanded her to stay there. Then I got what I needed from my laboratory, having in the meantime thought of trying to float medicine and other things to you down Lost River in brass cylinders, provided I should fail to reach you by airplane. It all depended on whether Lost River actually ran underground to the Valley of Arcana. I knew that it was snowing hard in the mountains, but that it was too late for me to get in afoot.

"I was fortunate in being able to hire a government monoplane, but the pilot was doubtful about the mountain blizzards from the outset. However, he was game and willing to do his best, and we set out hopefully.

"In a surprisingly short time the mountains were below us, and I thought of all the hardships you and I had gone through in covering the same distance. But the storms were raging; we could see almost nothing of the land beneath us. It was impossible to make a landing anywhere, but when a blizzard caught us we made one nevertheless.

"I thought my last day had come when we swooped down at terrific speed. But the pilot regained control of the thing, and, though we could not rise again, we came down much more slowly. We landed in a snowdrift high up in the mountains, and my pilot was knocked senseless, having struck his head on something in the fall. I was completely unhurt.

"I was a long time locating ourselves. I had to work alone, because Lieutenant Cantenwine, the pilot, was helpless. But finally, wandering about, I came upon a streak through the forest where trees had been felled and brush cut, indicating a trail under the snow. I followed it, and it led me to an Indian village.

"I had stumbled upon the reservation that Henry told us about at Shirttail Bend. The Indians were kind and readily offered to help me. The entire tribe, I believe, accompanied me back to Cantenwine and the airplane. It was the biggest day in their lives.

"They carried the lieutenant to the reservation on a stretcher, where I put him to bed. His skull is not fractured, but he has had a terrible shaking-up and was out of business. I had no way of knowing whether the plane was damaged or not, for I know nothing about airplanes. So I paid no attention to that, but next day questioned the Indians about Lost River, and was told that the source of it was not many miles away. They offered to take me to it on snowshoes, and we set out early through a driving storm.

"We reached it, and, with the awed natives standing about, I launched two of the cylinders. Two days later I went again with a guide and launched the third. Since then I have spent the greater part of my time doctoring Cantenwine and, since the weather has cleared, watching for the second stream of smoke, which never rose.

"The lieutenant is about now and has examined the airplane. It is not damaged beyond repair, and he is at work on it. He hopes to be able to make another attempt to reach the Valley of Arcana in a few days, if the weather continues to clear. We will circle over the valley, when we locate it, and try to make a landing on the lake. It must be frozen over, and we think that the high winds that have been blowing ought to clear the ice of snow. If not, landing will be a serious matter; but we hope for the best.

"This is all, Charmian, and I hope fervently that God will direct this message into your hands. Your single stream of smoke tells me that you are alive, and I thank Him for that. If Andy is in the condition that I think he is, you will realize now that you can never marry him. Even though we are able to bring him back to his old buoyant self, marriage is out of the question for him. He has no right to bring children into the world, which may be cretins, as he is. Knowing him as I do, I feel sure that, when he realizes his condition, he will give you up to me if it kills him. Poor Andy! I know that this must be a bitter blow to you, and I am sorry. But you must be told the truth now, and Andy must know too. If he comes back before we reach you, tell him everything.

"God bless you and help you.

"Devotedly,
"INMAN SHONTO."

For a long time after reading the message Charmian sat staring at the fire. Absent-mindedly she opened the packages—found tablets, coffee, sugar—all dry. Then she suddenly realized that she was growing cold again, and rose to put on such dry clothes as she could find. With these on, and the blanket again wrapped about her, she went out in a sort of stupor and built a second signal fire about a hundred feet from the first. She returned to the cave and seated herself again, drying her clothes before the blaze. She was stunned, stupid. She could not think. It was the cold, she told herself. Everything was all right now. Inman Shonto would come to her soon. She would hear a human voice again—his voice!

Her chin sank to her breast and she fell sound asleep sitting upright before the fire.

Days had passed—how many Charmian Reemy did not know—before she heard the hum of the airplane in the sky above the Valley of Arcana. Another storm had raged since she had received the doctor's message, and the mystic snow banners had streamed above the sink from the surrounding peaks. She had realized that it was impossible for him to reach her under these conditions, and had bravely submitted to the inevitable. Daily she cooked and ate her simple food. How delightful was the coffee! Daily she gave the cretin his tablet—forced it between his swollen lips and washed it down his throat with water, often nearly choking him.

Gradually the miracle took place. Slowly but surely the film left the eyes of the sufferer, and day by day they brightened. The swelling left the protruding tongue. The sallowness departed from the skin. The flabbiness departed. The lips became dry and firm. The asthmatic wheeze was gone from his breathing. The bloated, baglike abdomen receded. The light of reason came back in his eyes, and he drew in his protruding tongue repeatedly, glancing shame-facedly at Charmian to see if she had observed.

He smiled at her. He began to mumble. Then words came, and finally simple, broken sentences expressing the sufferer's wants.

He was at this stage when the snow ceased falling. Two days of calm were followed by a bitter wind, which cut the snow from the hillsides and sent

Charmian struggling to a lofty eminence from where she had a view of the distant ice-locked lake.

She could see the snow clouds blowing over there, and her heart leaped with hope. Then the airplane came roaring over the valley, circled down into it, glided to one end of the lake, turned, and came on in a downward swoop with the stretch of ice before it. She saw it strike the ice and held her breath. Great clouds of snow-dust arose and hit it, and she screamed with dread. But next instant she saw it skimming over the ice at terrific speed, the snow clouds trailing behind it. Slower and slower became its rate of progress; and when it was still Charmian sank down in the snow, and for the first time since reading the doctor's message she found relief in tears.

She stood up after the storm of tears had passed and saw two tiny figures coming toward her over the snow. She watched them, fascinated, for over half an hour, insensible to the biting wind. Then when they drew nearer she noted that they were headed toward her smoke streams, and she jumped about and waved her arms to attract attention to herself.

Presently she knew that they had seen her, for the foremost waved his hat and the two changed direction. The speed at which they travelled showed that they were on snowshoes. They come on rapidly straight toward her. Then when they were very near and she heard a faint shout and recognized the doctor's voice, a sudden wild panic seized her. She had been alone so long in that wild, desolate snow land, with only a helpless, drivelling idiot for company, that a strange dread of meeting these men took hold on her. Again the doctor shouted to her. Hysteria overcame her. With a little moan she turned and started running like a wild thing toward her cave.

Three times she stumbled over rocks hidden in the snow and pitched forward on her face. She had left the knoll and was on the level land. She glanced back over her shoulder as she ran. It seemed that no one was pursuing her. She slackened her pace, stopped, trembling and sobbing, and tried to fight off her terror.

And then it was that a figure suddenly stood before her with two arms outstretched. She had not realized that they would not follow her over the knoll, but would keep to the level land and travel much faster than she had. They even had passed her, and had cut in ahead of her.

She shrank back, biting her white lips.

"There—there—there!" came in soothing tones. "It's all right now—all right now, Charmian."

Next instant the long arms closed about her. Her tears burst forth again, but she lowered her head to Inman Shonto's shoulder, and the panic passed.

"There—there—there!"—as soft as the voice of a mother bending over the cradle of her child.

She looked up, dark eyes swimming. There came a smile—a little up-flirt at one corner of her mouth.

Without reserve he lowered his lips to hers and kissed her tenderly, as if all along he had known that this precious moment would one day come to him.

"It's all right now—all right now, Charmian."

And Charmian knew that it was all right now.

Two hours later the great man-made bird rose from the ice-sheet on the lake and roared away over the Valley of Arcana—away from the ice and snow and the horrors of the rocky cave—away to the sunny green lands that border the blue Pacific.

And the little ouzel, lifting his fluty notes amidst the icy spray of his beloved waterfall, bobbed and bowed and dived happily, and knew not of its going.

THE END

Milton Keynes UK
Ingram Content Group UK Ltd.
UKHW030741071024
449371UK00006B/674